AI FUSION

TRANSFORMING THE DIGITAL WORLD

A SYMPHONY OF MINDS & MACHINES

KISHOR NARAYANAN CHIYYARATH

ISBN

Paperback 979-8-89699-795-5
Hardcase 979-8-89929-907-0

Dedication

To my beloved wife, **Suju**, for her unwavering support, love, and encouragement.

To my wonderful children, **Abhiram** and **Aakash**, who inspire me every day with their curiosity and enthusiasm for learning.

To my dear **Achan** and **Amma**, whose wisdom and guidance have shaped the person I am today.

To my brothers & Sisters, for their constant support and belief in my journey.

And to my incredible colleagues and co-workers, whose collaboration, dedication, and shared passion for excellence have been instrumental in every milestone of this journey.

This book is for all of you, my pillars of strength and inspiration.

Contents

Preface

In today's fast-paced digital era, the convergence of artificial intelligence (AI) and digital transformation is no longer just a concept of the future; it's our present reality. From reshaping industries and elevating customer experiences to redefining workplace dynamics, AI has firmly integrated itself into the core of modern business strategies. This transformative journey has inspired me to pen *AI Fusion: Transforming the Digital World - A Symphony of Minds & Machine*, a book that delves into the opportunities and complexities of AI-driven digital transformation.

AI is now accessible to organizations of all sizes, offering tools to streamline processes, innovate solutions, and create sustainable growth. However, the fusion of AI and human intelligence—this symphony of minds and machines—presents both profound opportunities and significant challenges. How do we ensure that our digital transformation initiatives not only drive efficiency but also align with broader societal goals? How do we navigate the ethical dilemmas and prepare our workforce for this new era?

Throughout the book, I aim to provide practical insights into these questions. With over two decades of experience leading technology transition projects, I have witnessed firsthand the impact that strategic planning, clear vision, and a human-centered approach can have on digital transformation success. I explore how AI can be a force for good, promoting sustainable innovation and operational excellence, while addressing the ethical and socio-economic implications that come with it.

Each chapter of this book unpacks a different aspect of the AI journey, covering everything from ethical AI practices and data-driven decision-making to emerging trends and real-world case studies. My hope is that this book will serve as a roadmap for leaders, entrepreneurs, and anyone keen on navigating the evolving landscape of AI-powered digital transformation.

The path ahead is filled with potential but also with responsibilities. I invite you to join me in exploring how we can make the most of this digital symphony, embracing AI as not just a tool, but a partner in building a more sustainable and inclusive future.

Kishor Narayanan Chiyyarath
January 2025

1
Introduction

"The future belongs to those who embrace the harmony between human intelligence and artificial innovation."

In the digital age, change is no longer a distant concept—it's an ongoing reality that businesses must embrace to remain relevant. Artificial intelligence (AI) has evolved from a futuristic notion to a critical driver of digital transformation, reshaping industries, and redefining how organizations operate, interact, and grow. Yet, while the potential of AI is vast, the journey to successful digital transformation is fraught with obstacles. Studies show that nearly 70% of digital transformation projects fail, primarily due to a lack of strategic direction and an inability to fully integrate AI into organizational culture. The *Symphony of Minds and Machines*, as I call it, is not just about implementing AI but about achieving harmony between human intelligence and AI capabilities to unlock the true potential of digital transformation.

Understanding the Symphony: Minds and Machines in Harmony

The concept of AI Fusion—the blend of human ingenuity with machine intelligence—lies at the heart of effective digital transformation. When we talk about the *Symphony of Minds and Machines*, we're envisioning a seamless collaboration where AI amplifies human capabilities, and humans guide AI with strategic insight. AI is not just a tool; it is a partner in the transformation process, enabling businesses to process data, make informed decisions, and automate processes at unprecedented speeds.

The human mind is adept at critical thinking, creativity, and ethical judgment, while machines excel at processing vast amounts of data, detecting patterns, and performing repetitive tasks with precision. Together, they create a harmonious synergy, a symphony where each element complements the other, fostering a balanced, effective, and sustainable digital transformation. This symphony isn't achieved by simply deploying AI technologies—it requires a thoughtful approach that leverages both human and machine strengths.

The Current Landscape of Digital Transformation

To understand the role of AI in digital transformation, we must first recognize the trends and forces currently shaping this landscape:

- **The Explosion of Data**: Data is the lifeblood of AI, and in today's world, it is being generated at an exponential rate. IDC estimates that by 2025, the global datasphere will reach 175 zettabytes, a figure so large it's almost unimaginable. Organizations that harness AI to analyze and act on this data can gain unprecedented insights into customer behaviors, operational efficiencies, and market trends. Yet, many companies struggle with data overload, lacking the tools and strategies to convert raw data into actionable insights.

- **AI-Driven Automation**: Automation is a key driver of efficiency in the digital age, and AI takes this to new heights by enabling automation that is not only fast but also intelligent. According to a McKinsey report, AI could automate up to 45% of work activities, which translates into cost savings, productivity gains, and the freeing of human talent for strategic tasks. In industries ranging from manufacturing to customer service, AI-powered automation is helping businesses streamline operations and improve accuracy.

- **Customer Expectations and Personalization**: In a world where customers demand instant, personalized experiences, AI enables businesses to deliver tailored solutions at scale. According to Salesforce, 62% of customers expect companies to anticipate their needs. AI-driven personalization allows organizations to understand customer preferences and deliver experiences that not only meet but exceed expectations. Companies like Amazon and Netflix have set the bar high with AI-driven recommendation engines that keep users engaged and loyal.

- **Enhanced Cybersecurity**: As organizations become more digital, they also become more vulnerable to cyber threats. Gartner predicts that by 2025, AI-driven cybersecurity solutions will be essential for protecting digital assets. AI helps organizations detect threats in real-time, respond to incidents with agility, and safeguard sensitive information, making it a cornerstone of resilient digital transformation strategies.

- **AI and Innovation**: AI is not just a tool for optimization; it's a catalyst for innovation. From developing new products to pioneering cutting-edge technologies, AI empowers businesses to explore possibilities that were once confined to the realm of science fiction. In healthcare, AI-driven diagnostics and personalized medicine are transforming patient care, while in finance, AI is revolutionizing risk assessment and fraud detection.

Why Digital Transformation Projects Often Fail

Despite the immense potential of AI and digital transformation, many projects fail to deliver the expected outcomes. Research indicates that this high failure rate is often due to a lack of strategic alignment. Companies jump into digital transformation without a clear understanding of their objectives or a well-defined strategy. They treat AI as a silver bullet rather than as a component of a holistic approach to business transformation. Here are some common pitfalls:

- **Lack of a Defined Purpose**: Many organizations start digital transformation initiatives without fully understanding why they need to transform. They adopt AI tools without a clear vision of how these technologies will support their goals. Without a well-defined purpose, these projects often lose momentum and fail to achieve meaningful results.

- **Underestimating the Human Element**: Digital transformation is not just about technology—it's about people. Organizations that overlook the importance of culture, training, and change management often face resistance from employees, leading to low adoption rates and missed opportunities. Successful transformation requires a culture that embraces change, continuous learning, and a willingness to innovate.

- **Failure to Integrate AI into the Core Strategy**: AI should be an integral part of a company's strategic plan, not an afterthought. Projects often fail when organizations treat AI as a separate initiative rather than as a core component of their overall strategy. Integration requires a clear roadmap, adequate resources, and a commitment to aligning AI with business goals.

AI Fusion: Crafting a Symphony for Digital Success

Throughout this book, we will explore how *AI Fusion*—the harmonious integration of AI and human capabilities—creates a pathway to successful digital transformation. This isn't about simply implementing AI tools; it's about weaving AI into the fabric of your organization, where it enhances decision-making, drives efficiency, and supports innovation. Each of the 21 chapters that follow will focus into a specific aspect of AI-driven transformation, from leveraging big data and enhancing customer experience to building ethical AI frameworks and exploring the future of work.

By drawing on real-world examples, best practices, and cutting-edge research, this book provides a roadmap for businesses looking to harness the power of AI to stay competitive, resilient, and innovative. Whether you are just beginning your digital transformation journey or looking to refine an existing strategy, the insights shared here will help you navigate the complexities of AI Fusion and unlock the full potential of the symphony between minds and machines.

As we set out on this journey together, keep in mind that successful digital transformation is more than a technological upgrade—it's a fundamental shift in how businesses operate, engage with customers, and create value. In the chapters ahead, you will discover how AI can be a powerful ally in this transformation, helping you to build a future where human ingenuity and machine intelligence work together in perfect harmony.

Final Thoughts: As we've seen, the integration of AI into digital transformation is not just about implementing new technologies; it's about synchronizing human intellect with machine intelligence to create a harmonious and powerful symphony. AI Fusion represents the next frontier where businesses can innovate, adapt, and thrive by leveraging AI's capabilities to enhance human decision-making, creativity, and operational efficiency. In an age where rapid change is the only constant, organizations that align their strategies with the transformative power of AI will be poised for success.

Looking Ahead: In the chapters that follow, we'll dive deeper into various aspects of AI-driven digital transformation. From exploring how AI is revolutionizing customer experiences to understanding the ethical considerations of AI deployment, each chapter will illuminate a different facet of this dynamic journey. As we delve into these topics, you'll gain insights into not only how to harness AI for digital transformation but also how to navigate the challenges and seize the opportunities that lie ahead.

Let's embark on this journey together to discover how AI and human ingenuity are transforming the digital world, setting the stage for a future where innovation and ethics coalesce to redefine what's possible.

2

The AI Revolution: Catalyzing Digital Transformation

"AI isn't just changing technology—it's redefining how industries evolve and adapt."

In the fast-paced world of technology, change is no longer just on the horizon—it's already here. Artificial intelligence (AI) is no longer something we talk about in the future tense. Today, AI is the driving force behind digital transformation, pushing businesses to innovate at breakneck speed, make smarter decisions, and stay competitive in an ever-evolving marketplace.

Digital Transformation in the Age of AI

Digital transformation has been a buzzword for some time, but its meaning has evolved. At its core, digital transformation is about integrating digital technologies into every aspect of a business, fundamentally reshaping how organizations operate and deliver value. But when AI enters the picture, the pace of this transformation accelerates. AI isn't just another digital tool—it's an intelligent system capable of learning, predicting, and automating tasks that were once beyond the reach of machines.

From AI-powered customer service chatbots to advanced data analytics platforms, AI has infiltrated almost every industry. It's not only helping businesses become more efficient—it's fundamentally changing how they grow, evolve, and prepare for the future. Companies that embrace AI aren't just upgrading their processes; they're redefining what business success looks like.

What's Fueling the AI Revolution?

Several key factors are driving AI's rapid adoption in the digital transformation strategies of today's leading businesses:

- **Data Explosion**: In the digital age, data is everywhere—produced by consumers, businesses, and devices at a staggering rate. AI thrives on this data, enabling businesses to uncover insights that were once hidden in plain sight. With AI, companies can gain a deeper understanding of customer behaviors, market trends, and operational efficiencies, empowering them to make smarter decisions.

- **Automation**: One of AI's most significant contributions to digital transformation is automation. AI-powered automation helps businesses streamline their operations, from supply chain management to routine administrative tasks. By automating these processes, companies can cut costs, improve accuracy, and increase productivity—all while freeing up their teams to focus on more creative and strategic work.

- **AI-Driven Innovation**: AI isn't just making existing processes faster or more efficient—it's opening doors to entirely new possibilities. Whether it's developing personalized products, enhancing customer experiences, or enabling precision in healthcare, AI is helping businesses rethink their approach to innovation.

- **Customer Expectations**: Today's consumers demand fast, personalized, and seamless experiences. AI allows companies to anticipate customer needs, deliver tailored services, and continuously improve satisfaction—all at scale. The result? Happier, more loyal customers who feel understood and valued.

AI: The New Engine of Digital Transformation

When we talk about digital transformation, we often think about cloud computing, mobile applications, and social media platforms.

While these technologies still play a vital role, AI has emerged as the new engine powering the next level of transformation.

AI doesn't just enable businesses to make digital upgrades—it transforms how they operate at their core. Consider the case of **predictive maintenance in manufacturing**. With AI, machines can now detect potential issues before they become major problems, allowing businesses to minimize downtime and save on repair costs. Or think about **AI in finance**, where real-time fraud detection and personalized financial services offer customers a safer and more customized experience.

In short, AI is not just another tool in the digital transformation toolkit—it's the game-changer that propels businesses into new, uncharted territory. Companies that successfully harness AI are able to process vast amounts of data, make faster and more informed decisions, and build a stronger foundation for the future.

Success Stories: How AI Is Transforming Industries

AI-driven digital transformation is already delivering impressive results across industries. Here are a few early success stories:

- **Healthcare**: AI is revolutionizing healthcare, from predictive diagnostics to personalized treatments. Companies like IBM Watson Health are using AI to analyze vast datasets, helping doctors spot patterns and make faster, more accurate decisions.

- **Retail**: E-commerce giants like Amazon leverage AI to offer personalized product recommendations, creating more engaging customer experiences and driving revenue.

AI-powered logistics and supply chain management systems also help streamline operations and reduce delivery times.

- **Finance**: In the financial sector, AI-driven robo-advisors, fraud detection systems, and personalized financial products are transforming how banks interact with customers and manage risk.

These examples show that companies embracing AI as part of their digital transformation strategies are not just improving what they do—they're completely redefining how they operate and engage with their customers.

From Reactive to Proactive: A Shift in Strategy

In the early days of digital transformation, businesses were often reactive—using digital tools to respond to customer needs or market changes as they arose. But with AI, companies can take a proactive approach. Instead of reacting to problems, AI allows businesses to predict future trends, automate decision-making, and anticipate customer needs with unprecedented accuracy.

This shift—from reactive to proactive—is the next phase of digital transformation. AI isn't just a supporting actor in this transformation—it's taking center stage as the core driver of innovation and operational excellence.

Final Thoughts: As AI continues to evolve, it's clear that it will drive the next wave of digital transformation. Businesses that adopt AI-driven solutions early are already gaining an edge, automating more efficiently, innovating faster, and staying ahead of their competition. For those looking to thrive in the digital age, embracing AI is no longer optional—it's essential.

Looking Ahead: The AI revolution is here, and those who take advantage of it will lead the way in shaping the digital world of tomorrow. As we move forward into the next chapters, we'll dive deeper into how AI is transforming specific areas of business and what it means for the future of work, sustainability, and beyond.

3

Understanding the Fusion: AI and Human Collaboration

"When human creativity meets artificial intelligence, the possibilities become limitless."

In the previous chapter, we explored how artificial intelligence (AI) is driving the digital transformation of industries. But as we dig deeper, one of the most fascinating aspects of this transformation is the evolving relationship between humans and machines. AI is no longer just a tool that we use—it's becoming a partner that works alongside us, augmenting our abilities and enabling us to achieve more than we ever thought possible. This chapter will dive into the dynamic fusion of human intelligence and AI, and how this collaboration is shaping the future of work and innovation.

The Symbiotic Relationship Between Humans and AI

For years, there's been a fear that AI will replace humans in the workforce. Headlines warning of robots taking over jobs have stirred anxiety across industries. But the reality is more nuanced. AI isn't here to replace us—it's here to amplify what we can do. When humans and AI work together, we create something far more powerful than either could achieve alone.

This fusion is already evident in industries ranging from healthcare to finance. In medicine, for instance, AI can analyze vast amounts of data, identifying patterns and offering insights that even the most experienced doctors might miss. But AI doesn't replace the doctor—it assists. The human touch, the doctor's judgment, and their ability to communicate with patients are irreplaceable. Together, AI and humans deliver better outcomes than either could alone.

In finance, AI systems can scan millions of transactions in real time to detect fraud. However, when it comes to complex decisions—like approving a loan or managing investment portfolios—human intuition and experience remain critical. AI provides the data-driven insights, and humans provide the ethical judgment and strategic thinking.

AI as an Enabler of Human Potential

So, what does AI do that makes this partnership so effective? At its core, AI handles the tasks that humans find tedious, time-consuming, or too vast to manage on their own. This frees us to focus on areas where human skills shine—creativity, problem-solving, empathy, and innovation.

Let's think about creative industries, like marketing or design. AI can analyze market trends, customer behaviors, and competitive landscapes at speeds that humans can't match. It can suggest optimal strategies based on data. But it's the humans who add the creative flair—the ideas, the emotional resonance, the unique perspectives that turn data into impactful campaigns.

The same is true in product development. AI might optimize the design process, suggesting improvements based on previous successes or failures. But it's the human teams that come up with the vision for what the product should be, how it should feel, and how it can solve real-world problems.

By handling repetitive or data-heavy tasks, AI allows humans to work smarter, not harder. It unlocks the potential for more creativity, more strategic thinking, and ultimately, more innovation.

AI and Human Collaboration in Action

Real-world examples highlight how AI-human collaboration is making an impact:

- **Healthcare**: As discussed in the previous chapter, AI is being used to assist doctors in diagnosing diseases more accurately. In radiology, for instance, AI-powered imaging tools can detect abnormalities in scans that the human eye might miss. But the final diagnosis is still made by a human doctor, who weighs AI's insights alongside their own knowledge and patient context.

- **Customer Service**: AI-powered chatbots are handling basic customer inquiries, freeing up human agents to focus on more complex problems. The result? Customers get faster service, and human agents have more time to deliver personalized, high-value interactions.

- **Manufacturing**: In smart factories, AI systems monitor production lines, predicting equipment failures before they happen. Human engineers, armed with this data, can then make informed decisions on maintenance schedules and system improvements.

In these examples, AI doesn't replace the human role—it enhances it. By collaborating with AI, humans can make better decisions, faster, and focus on the aspects of their work that add the most value.

Trusting the AI Partner

For this collaboration to work effectively, there's one key ingredient: trust. If humans don't trust AI, they won't fully embrace it as a partner. Building trust in AI means ensuring transparency, reliability, and ethics in how AI systems operate.

For example, in the financial sector, AI algorithms that determine loan eligibility must be transparent in how decisions are made. If customers believe that AI is making unfair or biased decisions, trust is eroded. Therefore, transparency—knowing how AI arrives at its conclusions—is critical for building trust between humans and machines.

Organizations that implement AI systems must also prioritize ethics. AI must be programmed to make decisions that are fair and unbiased, especially when those decisions affect people's lives—whether it's hiring, lending, or healthcare. Trustworthy AI systems will enhance human collaboration and open the door to even greater possibilities.

Final Thoughts: As AI continues to evolve, so too will our collaboration with it. The future of work won't be about humans or AI working in isolation—it will be about a seamless partnership where AI enhances human abilities and enables us to work smarter and more creatively.

In the near future, we may see even more integrated systems where AI assists with real-time decision-making. For instance, AI could offer surgeons instant data analysis during operations or provide real-time feedback to teachers based on student engagement levels in classrooms. The possibilities are endless, but the underlying principle remains the same: humans and AI are better together.

The real opportunity in the AI age isn't about competing with machines; it's about learning to collaborate with them. Those who can leverage AI as a partner will be the ones who succeed in the digital transformation journey.

Looking Ahead: As we move into the next chapter, we'll explore one of the key enablers of this collaboration: data. Data fuels AI's ability to assist and enhance human decision-making. In Chapter 4, we'll dive into how data collection, analysis, and management play a critical role in successful AI-driven digital transformation.

4

Fueling AI Transformation: Data & Computing Power

"Data fuels intelligence, but computing power ignites transformation."

In the previous chapter, we explored how AI and human collaboration are transforming industries. But there's an essential component that powers AI and makes these innovations possible— data. Data is the fuel that drives AI, and without it, AI would be an engine without gas. In this chapter, we'll dive into why data is the foundation of AI, how organizations can harness it effectively, and what the future of data management looks like in an AI-powered world.

Why Data Matters in the AI Age

AI's ability to "think" and "learn" depends entirely on the data it is fed. Without data, AI cannot generate insights, make predictions, or automate decisions. In essence, data is the lifeblood of artificial intelligence, and the more high-quality data AI systems have, the better they perform.

Take a moment to think about how often you interact with AI-driven services. Every time you ask your virtual assistant for a weather update, scroll through personalized recommendations on a shopping site, or receive an alert about your spending habits from your bank, data is at work. Every click, search, and transaction generates valuable data, which AI processes to provide you with tailored experiences.

But it's not just about quantity—quality of data is crucial. Feeding AI irrelevant, outdated, or incomplete data can lead to poor decisions and unreliable results. As AI continues to advance, businesses must invest in collecting, curating, and managing high-quality data to unlock the full potential of AI.

Big Data: The Power Behind AI

The term Big Data often gets thrown around, but what does it really mean, and why is it so important for AI? Big Data refers to the vast volumes of data generated every second—from social media posts and online transactions to sensor data from connected devices. It's called "big" not just because of the sheer amount of data but also because of its complexity and variety.

AI thrives on Big Data because it provides the raw material needed for learning and improving over time. The more data AI has to work with, the better it can identify patterns, make accurate predictions, and evolve its capabilities. This is why tech giants like Google, Amazon, and Meta (formerly Facebook) are at the forefront of AI innovation—they have access to an unprecedented amount of data.

Meta, for example, uses vast datasets from its social platforms like Facebook and Instagram to power its recommendation algorithms. These systems analyze user behavior, preferences, and interactions to deliver personalized content and advertisements tailored to individual users. Such large datasets also help in training its AI systems for applications like **Horizon Workrooms**, a VR collaboration tool where AI assists in virtual interactions and spatial recognition.

The Demand for Massive Computing Power

Modern AI models, especially deep learning frameworks like transformers, require enormous computational resources. The complexity stems from the billions—or even trillions—of parameters involved in large models such as GPT-4 and Google's

PaLM. These models require extensive **CPU (Central Processing Units)** and **GPU (Graphics Processing Units)** power for both training and inference phases.

Why Computing Power Matters:

- **Model Depth and Complexity:** Larger models require significantly more FLOPs (Floating Point Operations) to train effectively.

- **Parallel Processing Needs:** AI models rely on high-performance GPUs capable of parallel computations across thousands of cores.

- **Training Time:** Some of the largest language models require weeks or months of continuous training on specialized supercomputers.

Example: OpenAI's **GPT-4** was trained using thousands of **NVIDIA A100 GPUs** in parallel, processing massive datasets for weeks. This infrastructure demand often results in substantial operational costs and environmental impact.

The Challenge of Training Data at Scale

The effectiveness of an AI model is directly tied to the quality and volume of its training data. As models scale, datasets often reach **trillions of data points**, presenting unique challenges:

- **Storage and Management:** Storing massive datasets requires highly scalable cloud architectures or distributed storage solutions.

- **Processing Speed:** Loading, preprocessing, and training on large datasets demands significant memory and high-bandwidth data pipelines.

- **Quality vs. Quantity:** More data doesn't always equal better results. Low-quality data can introduce biases and errors into the model.

Example: Training an **image recognition model** on datasets like **ImageNet** involves processing millions of high-resolution images, demanding petabytes of storage and powerful **tensor processing units (TPUs)** for efficient handling.

The Risk of AI Hallucinations

As models grow larger and more complex, the phenomenon of **AI hallucinations** becomes increasingly relevant. **AI hallucination** refers to instances where an AI model generates incorrect or nonsensical information despite being trained on vast datasets.

Why Hallucinations Occur

- **Overfitting:** When the model memorizes patterns from the training data instead of generalizing, leading to unreliable outputs.

- **Incomplete Data Representation:** If the data lacks diversity or is skewed, the model may generate inaccurate results.

- **Training Artifacts:** Spurious correlations in the data can cause models to infer patterns that do not exist.

Example: Meta's **BlenderBot**, a conversational AI, faced issues where it fabricated responses when handling complex queries due to incomplete or biased training data.

Addressing AI Hallucinations

- **Dataset Expansion and Curation:** Using diverse, well-annotated datasets to improve generalization.

- **Regularization Techniques:** Applying techniques like dropout and batch normalization to reduce overfitting.

- **Human-in-the-Loop Verification:** Involving human reviewers to validate the model's outputs, especially in critical applications.

Edge Computing: A Game-Changer in AI Transformation

While massive datasets and large-scale computing power are essential for training complex AI models, **edge computing** offers an innovative solution for handling data more efficiently during inference and real-time decision-making.

Edge computing involves processing data **closer to its source** (at the "edge" of the network) rather than relying on centralized cloud data centers. This decentralized approach minimizes the need for continuous data transfers, reducing latency and bandwidth requirements.

Why Edge Computing Matters for AI

- **Reduced Latency:** Edge devices can process data in near real-time, which is critical for applications like **autonomous vehicles** and **video analytics** in smart cities.

- **Bandwidth Efficiency:** Since less data is transmitted back to the cloud, edge computing helps optimize bandwidth usage, especially for video analytics where data volume is extremely high.

- **Enhanced Privacy:** Sensitive data can be processed locally, reducing the risks associated with transmitting personal data over networks.

- **Energy Savings:** Offloading tasks to local devices can reduce the energy footprint compared to relying on massive data centers.

Example: Edge Computing in Video Analytics

Consider a **smart surveillance system** deployed across a city. Traditional video analytics require streaming all video feeds to a central server for processing, which consumes extensive bandwidth and requires powerful cloud infrastructure.

With **Edge Computing**, AI models for object detection and anomaly tracking can be deployed directly on **edge devices** like NVIDIA Jetson modules placed on-site. These devices can process data locally, sending only **critical alerts** and summarized information to the central server, improving both speed and efficiency.

How Edge Computing Balances the Computing Power Challenge

In the context of **AI Transformation**, edge computing serves as a powerful **complement** to centralized cloud infrastructure:

- **Training AI Models:** Large models still require **high-performance GPUs and TPUs** in centralized data centers for training.

- **Deploying AI Models:** Once trained, models can be **compressed** and deployed on edge devices for faster real-time decision-making.

- **Hybrid Approach:** A hybrid infrastructure using both **cloud-based training** and **edge-based inference** can offer a scalable solution for AI applications.

Edge Computing's Role in Preventing AI Hallucinations

Edge computing can also help address **AI hallucinations** by ensuring **localized data validation** before decisions are made. Since edge devices work with smaller, more contextually relevant datasets, they can minimize the risks of models generating misleading or irrelevant information due to incomplete data.

Balancing Power, Data, and Sustainability

While the need for **computing power** and **large datasets** continues to grow, balancing performance with **sustainability** is crucial:

- **Energy-Efficient Hardware:** Using specialized chips like **TPUs** designed for AI workloads to reduce power consumption.

- **Distributed Training:** Splitting workloads across multiple nodes to optimize resource usage.

- **Green AI Practices:** Minimizing energy waste by training models with smaller, optimized datasets when possible.

Final Thoughts: Computing power and data quality are foundational to successful AI implementation. As data grows in complexity and models demand more resources, organizations must prioritize **efficient infrastructure** and **ethical data use**. By incorporating Edge Computing alongside high-performance computing resources and big data strategies, organizations can create a balanced AI infrastructure. This hybrid approach ensures:

- Scalability without compromising speed.

- Sustainable data practices.

- Reduced infrastructure costs while maintaining performance.

Balancing power, performance, and sustainability will be key for the future of responsible AI-driven transformation.

Looking Ahead: As we transition to Chapter 5, we'll dive deeper into the essential components of a digital transformation framework. We'll explore how strategy, organizational alignment, and change management form the backbone of a successful digital transformation. With AI as a driving force, this framework enables organizations to assess digital maturity, overcome barriers, and navigate the complexities of today's digital landscape. Get ready to build a solid foundation for your AI-driven transformation journey

5
The Digital Transformation Framework

*"A successful transformation is built on strategy,
alignment, and continuous growth."*

Digital transformation is all the rage these days, but here's a sobering fact: most digital transformation projects—up to 70% by some reports—fail. That's right. Despite the excitement and the endless possibilities, a majority of initiatives fall short of their goals. Why? Because too often, companies dive headfirst into the deep end without understanding what they really need or having a solid plan in place. In *AI Fusion: Transforming the Digital World*, I want to share a framework that addresses these pitfalls and outlines a pathway for success, one that's rooted in AI as the catalyst driving today's digital evolution.

Setting the Stage with a Solid Strategy

Let's start where it all begins: strategy. AI isn't just another tool; it's a game-changer. But to leverage it effectively, you need to align your AI initiatives with clear, purposeful objectives. Think of AI as a sophisticated engine that powers your digital transformation. Without a well-defined direction, even the most advanced AI can't deliver real value.

- **Identifying Real Needs**

  Before anything else, ask yourself: *What are we trying to achieve?* Whether it's improving customer engagement, automating processes, or unlocking new revenue streams, your goals need to be crystal clear. AI has immense potential, but it works best when it's solving a specific problem. Identify the pain points, prioritize them, and then align your AI strategy to tackle these issues head-on.

- **Defining Success Metrics that Matter**

  To gauge the impact of AI on your transformation journey, you need the right metrics. It's not just about implementing

AI for the sake of it; it's about achieving tangible results. Are you looking to enhance operational efficiency? Increase customer satisfaction? Boost profitability? Define KPIs that are directly tied to these objectives, so you can measure progress meaningfully and adjust as needed.

- **Tapping into Market and Tech Trends**

  In today's fast-paced world, what worked yesterday might not work tomorrow. Keeping an eye on industry trends and technological advancements is crucial. AI and digital transformation are constantly evolving fields, so understanding the competitive landscape can provide insights into where your efforts should be focused. Dive into current trends like generative AI, machine learning, and data analytics, and assess how they fit into your broader digital strategy.

Aligning Your Organization with AI at the Core

No transformation is possible without the people who make it happen. For AI-driven transformation to succeed, it needs to be a collective endeavor.

- **Getting Buy-In from Leadership**

  AI transformation isn't a solo act—it requires support from the top. Engage with your leadership and key stakeholders to ensure they understand AI's potential and are committed to the journey. Leaders who believe in the vision can drive change more effectively by securing resources, setting priorities, and fostering a culture that embraces innovation.

- **Breaking Down Silos with Cross-Functional Teams**

  AI thrives on collaboration. It's not just about one department or a single team; it's about the entire organization working together. By forming cross-functional teams, you can harness diverse perspectives, break down silos, and enable a more holistic approach to AI adoption. This collaborative spirit ensures that everyone is on the same page and invested in the outcome.

- **Empowering Your Workforce with AI Skills**

  The fear of AI replacing jobs is real, but it's only one side of the story. The other side? AI can also empower employees by enhancing their capabilities and freeing them from mundane tasks. Provide training and development opportunities to help your team adapt to AI tools and technologies. Encourage a growth mindset where AI is seen as an ally rather than a threat.

Managing Change: The Human Side of AI Transformation

Change is never easy, especially when it involves shifting mindsets and adopting new technologies. With AI, the challenge can feel even more daunting because it often touches multiple areas of a business—from how decisions are made to how employees perform their day-to-day tasks. This is where effective change management becomes essential. Embracing AI-driven transformation requires more than just technical adjustments; it calls for cultural shifts and a compassionate approach to guiding people through the change.

Planning for Change with Empathy

Every digital transformation initiative needs a clear roadmap that not only explains *how* things will change but also *why* these changes are happening. The key to success is connecting with your employees on a human level, explaining the purpose behind the transformation, and setting clear milestones to measure progress.

For instance, consider a healthcare organization implementing AI to optimize patient scheduling. Such a change might initially worry staff members who fear that automation will make their roles redundant. By explaining how AI will streamline processes to improve patient care, reduce wait times, and allow staff to focus on more meaningful interactions with patients, the organization can alleviate fears. Leaders can further build trust by holding workshops where employees can voice their concerns. When people feel heard and understand the broader benefits of the change, they are more likely to embrace it.

Staying Agile and Adaptive

AI itself is based on the principle of continuous learning and adaptation, and your approach to managing change should reflect this mindset. Flexibility is essential because, as with any significant change, there will inevitably be unexpected challenges. By staying agile, organizations can respond to real-time data, gather ongoing feedback, and be ready to pivot as necessary.

Imagine a retail company rolling out an AI-driven inventory management system. As employees begin using the new system, they might discover that certain processes, like handling returns, aren't as efficient as they had hoped. Instead of sticking rigidly to the original plan, the company could adopt an agile approach by collecting feedback, analyzing the data, and making real-time adjustments to improve the system. This might involve tweaking AI algorithms to better predict return volumes or adjusting the user interface to make it more intuitive. Remaining responsive in this way ensures that AI supports, rather than disrupts, the workflow.

The Role of Leadership in Managing Change

Leadership plays a crucial role in driving cultural change and making employees feel secure and motivated throughout the transformation. Leaders who model adaptability and openness to AI set a positive example for the rest of the organization, reinforcing the change and fostering a supportive environment.

Consider a financial services firm where AI is being introduced to improve fraud detection. Leaders can drive change by not only championing the new technology but also highlighting how it enhances the team's ability to catch fraudulent activities. Sharing success stories of employees who used AI insights to thwart significant fraud attempts can encourage others to embrace AI tools. By recognizing and rewarding those who adapt to new ways of working, leaders can further reinforce a culture that is open to AI-driven transformation.

Communicating the Vision Continuously

AI-driven transformation is not a one-time change; it's an ongoing journey that requires constant reinforcement. Regular communication helps keep the vision fresh and maintains momentum. Sharing updates on AI initiatives, celebrating small wins, and keeping everyone informed about the next steps in the journey can help sustain engagement over time.

In a tech company deploying AI to personalize user experiences, leaders might establish a weekly update email or a dashboard that shows how AI insights are enhancing customer satisfaction. This transparency helps employees see the direct impact of their efforts and understand the bigger picture. As they witness the positive effects of AI, they're more likely to support the ongoing transformation efforts.

Encouraging a Growth Mindset

Change is often resisted because it feels threatening, especially when it involves learning new skills. By encouraging a growth mindset, organizations can help employees see AI as an opportunity for professional development rather than a threat to their job security.

For example, a manufacturing company implementing AI to optimize production lines might offer workshops that train employees on how to use AI, while also highlighting the career benefits of AI proficiency. By framing AI as a tool that enhances their capabilities and opens doors to new opportunities, the organization can shift perspectives from fear to curiosity and enthusiasm.

In the end, managing change in AI-driven digital transformation is about guiding people through a journey of learning, adaptation, and growth. By planning with empathy, staying agile, and fostering a culture that embraces change, organizations can harness the full potential of AI while ensuring their workforce feels supported and empowered along the way.

Assessing Digital Maturity: Understanding Where You Stand

Before you can figure out where you're going, you need to know where you are. That's where digital maturity comes in. AI plays a huge role in scaling digital capabilities, but first, you need to assess your current level of digital maturity. This assessment will give you a clear picture of where your organization stands, reveal areas of strength, and highlight opportunities for improvement.

Using a Maturity Model to Benchmark Your Progress

A digital maturity model can help you assess your current capabilities and identify gaps. These models typically evaluate maturity across several dimensions, like data management, technology infrastructure, customer experience, and organizational culture. For example:

- **Deloitte's Digital Maturity Model** examines an organization's capabilities in areas like customer engagement, strategy, technology, and operations. Imagine a retail company using this model to find that while they excel at customer engagement, their data management systems are underdeveloped. This insight can lead them to invest in better data practices that support AI-driven customer insights and predictive analytics.

- **Boston Consulting Group's Digital Acceleration Index** can reveal where you stand in terms of digital culture, tech enablement, and innovation. Let's say a healthcare provider scores high on tech enablement but low on digital innovation. They might then prioritize building AI-driven predictive models to enhance patient care and stay competitive.

Assessing your digital maturity helps you understand if your organization is ready to leverage AI and where improvements are needed. Are your data management practices robust enough to support AI? Do you have the necessary infrastructure in place? Understanding your maturity level can reveal strengths and weaknesses, guiding you on where to invest time and resources.

Benchmarking Against Industry Peers

To gain a competitive edge, it's important to compare your digital capabilities with those of your peers. This is where industry benchmarking comes in. By understanding where you stand in relation to others, you can set realistic goals and avoid costly mistakes. AI can play a significant role here by providing insights from big data and predictive analytics.

For example:

- A financial services firm could use **Forrester's Digital Maturity Model** to benchmark itself against other players in the industry. They might find that while they are doing well in data security (essential for any financial institution), they lag in customer experience metrics compared to top competitors. This could drive them to focus on AI-driven personalization to enhance customer satisfaction.

- **Google's Digital Maturity Benchmark**, designed with digital marketing and customer experience in mind, can be a great tool for companies heavily invested in digital marketing. A company might discover that they're behind their peers in terms of data integration. This realization could prompt them to invest in AI-powered data integration tools that consolidate customer data across multiple channels, enabling a more personalized marketing approach.

Industry benchmarking offers a reality check. It reveals where you're excelling and where you might be lagging, allowing you to make informed decisions about where to focus AI-driven transformation efforts.

Setting Targets for Growth and Transformation

Once you know your digital maturity level, you can set ambitious yet achievable goals for AI-driven transformation. This means prioritizing areas for improvement, from technology adoption to customer experience, and charting a course that reflects both your vision and your readiness.

- For instance, a company using **Capgemini's Digital Maturity Model** may find that they need to work on their transformation management. They might then set a target to implement AI-driven project management tools that streamline workflows and enhance cross-functional collaboration.

- Or consider an organization that, through BCG's Digital Acceleration Index, identifies a gap in their digital leadership. They could set a goal to invest in AI training for their leadership team, ensuring that top decision-makers understand the technology's potential and limitations, and can advocate for its strategic use.

Setting targets based on digital maturity insights helps create a focused transformation roadmap. It allows you to prioritize initiatives that align with both your strategic goals and your current capabilities. With AI as an enabler, these targets become not just ambitious, but also attainable.

Final Thoughts: The framework outlined in this chapter is designed to demystify AI-driven digital transformation and provide a structured path to success. By aligning your strategy with clear goals, fostering a culture that embraces AI, managing change thoughtfully, and assessing your digital maturity, you can turn AI into a powerful ally in your journey toward a truly transformed digital world.

Looking Ahead: In the next chapter, we'll explore how the world of automation and innovation drives efficiency across various business functions. Building on our understanding of data's importance, we'll examine how AI leverages this data to streamline processes, reduce costs, and enhance productivity. Join with me in Chapter 6 as we uncover how AI-powered automation is not only transforming operations but also paving the way for innovative breakthroughs in business efficiency.

6
Automation and Innovation: AI's Role in Efficiency

"Automation isn't just about speed—it's about unlocking creativity and innovation."

Automation has quietly moved from the sidelines to center stage in today's business world. It's no longer just about cutting costs or speeding things up—it's about reimagining how work gets done. With AI now embedded in core operations, companies are shifting from manual, repetitive tasks to smart, self-optimizing systems. This evolution is helping businesses scale faster, respond quicker, and unlock new levels of creativity and competitiveness that simply weren't possible before. In this chapter, we'll dive into how **AI-driven automation** is transforming the way businesses operate and the long-term impact it has on productivity and growth.

The Age of AI-Driven Automation

AI-driven automation refers to the use of AI technologies to handle tasks that traditionally required human intervention. These tasks range from simple, repetitive activities like data entry to complex processes such as predictive analytics and decision-making. As companies face increasing demands to do more with less, AI is emerging as the key to unlocking new levels of efficiency.

According to **McKinsey's 2024–2025 Global AI Index**, organizations adopting AI at scale have seen **productivity improvements of 25–35%**, particularly in operations, customer service, and logistics. Automation is now deeply integrated into workflows, from supply chain management and customer service to manufacturing and finance. By allowing machines to take over routine tasks, businesses are not only improving efficiency but also enabling their human workforce to focus on more creative, strategic, and high-value activities.

How AI-Driven Automation Enhances Efficiency

At its core, AI automation is about **eliminating inefficiencies** in business processes. By leveraging AI algorithms and machine learning models, organizations can automate tasks that are time-consuming, error-prone, and repetitive. This shift has far-reaching implications for industries, as it allows companies to scale operations, reduce costs, and improve accuracy.

Here are some key ways AI-driven automation is enhancing efficiency across different sectors:

1. **Manufacturing and Supply Chains**: In the manufacturing sector, AI-driven automation is playing a pivotal role in improving production efficiency. AI-powered robots and automated machinery can work around the clock, increasing output while reducing the need for manual labor. AI is also transforming supply chains by optimizing inventory management, predicting demand, and identifying bottlenecks in the production process.

   In 2025, manufacturers are embracing AI to **optimize production lines**, minimize downtime, and manage inventory with unprecedented accuracy. AI-powered predictive maintenance is expected to reduce machine downtime by **up to 40%** (according to Siemens Industrial AI report 2025). **Capgemini's 2024 Smart Manufacturing Trends** report estimates that AI-enabled automation will **cut manufacturing operational costs by up to 22%** and boost throughput by **35%**, especially when integrated with IoT and digital twins.

2. **Customer Service**: AI chatbots and virtual assistants are becoming the face of customer service for many companies. These systems can handle customer inquiries 24/7, providing real-time responses to common questions and issues. This not only improves the customer experience but also reduces the workload for human agents, allowing them to focus on more complex queries.AI chatbots and virtual assistants are now handling **more than 80% of first-level support queries**, per **Gartner's 2025 AI in CX Study**. These AI agents are improving not only response time but customer satisfaction, with a **65% reduction in ticket resolution times** and **45–55% reduction in support costs**.The rise of multimodal AI—tools that can understand voice, text, and images—is making customer service more seamless and human-like

3. **Finance and Accounting**: In the financial sector, AI is being used to automate tasks such as invoice processing, fraud detection, and risk assessment. AI algorithms can analyze vast amounts of financial data in real time, identifying patterns and anomalies that would take humans hours or even days to process. This allows financial institutions to respond more quickly to emerging risks and opportunities. AI is taking over repetitive financial operations like **invoice matching, reconciliation, and fraud detection**. According to the **PwC 2024 Financial Automation Benchmark**, companies leveraging AI in finance report **a 50% increase in process accuracy** and **40% faster month-end closures**. Banks and fintech firms are deploying AI to handle **real-time risk assessments**

and credit scoring, enabling faster and more accurate decision-making

4. **Healthcare**: Healthcare is undergoing an AI-led transformation. From **predictive diagnostics** to **personalized treatment plans**, automation is saving time and lives. AI-powered systems can analyze medical records, lab results, and imaging scans faster than humans, allowing healthcare professionals to make informed decisions more quickly. For example, AI tools in radiology can detect early signs of diseases like cancer, leading to more timely treatments.According to **Accenture's 2025 Healthcare AI Outlook**, AI will help the global healthcare sector **save over $180 billion annually by 2026**, driven by improvements in workflow optimization, diagnostic accuracy, and patient monitoring. AI-powered radiology tools now assist in early detection of cancers and cardiovascular diseases, with diagnostic accuracy nearing **95% in controlled environments**

Innovation Through AI Automation

Beyond efficiency gains, AI-driven automation is also a catalyst for **innovation**. By automating routine tasks, companies can allocate more resources to research and development, leading to the creation of new products, services, and business models.

In **retail**, AI automation is transforming everything from inventory management to personalized marketing. Retailers are using AI to analyze customer behavior, predict trends, and create personalized shopping experiences. For instance, **Walmart** uses AI-driven automation in its warehouses to streamline inventory and reduce waste. This allows the company to focus on innovating customer experiences, such as developing new e-commerce platforms and enhancing same-day delivery services.

In **software development**, AI is helping developers write code faster and more efficiently by automating tasks such as bug detection, testing, and deployment. AI tools can generate code snippets, suggest improvements, and even write entire sections of code based on previous patterns. This automation frees developers to focus on creative problem-solving and innovation. According to **GitHub's 2024 Copilot Study**, developers using AI tools saw a **45% boost in productivity**, with code generation, testing, and debugging being the top automated areas.

The Long-Term Impact of AI-Driven Automation

The impact of AI automation on industries is profound, and its influence will only grow in the coming years. According to a **2024 World Economic Forum report**, by 2025, AI automation will have reshaped more than **85 million jobs** globally, creating new opportunities in sectors like data science, AI ethics, and automation engineering while displacing traditional roles that rely on repetitive, manual labor.

While automation has sparked concerns about job displacement, it's important to recognize that it also drives **job creation** in high-skill areas. Companies are investing in upskilling their workforce to prepare for the AI-driven future. In industries like **logistics** and **manufacturing**, workers are being trained to operate and maintain AI-powered systems, shifting from manual tasks to roles that require critical thinking and problem-solving.

For example, in **logistics**, AI is automating tasks like route optimization and inventory tracking, allowing companies to deliver goods more efficiently. While this reduces the need for traditional roles like warehouse clerks, it creates demand for new roles such as AI system operators and data analysts who oversee the automation systems. **McKinsey's 2023 Future of Work report** estimates that automation will lead to the creation of **133 million new jobs** by 2030, offsetting the displacement caused by AI.

Roles in AI ethics, automation oversight, human-AI collaboration, and digital operations management are on the rise. The **ILO 2024 report** emphasizes the importance of **reskilling**, noting that **companies investing in workforce transformation are 2.5 times more likely to be high-performing**

Overcoming Challenges in AI Automation

While AI automation offers immense benefits, it is not without its challenges. One of the key concerns is the **ethical implications** of AI replacing human jobs and the potential for **algorithmic bias**. To ensure that automation benefits everyone, companies must adopt responsible AI practices, such as auditing algorithms for fairness and transparency and involving human oversight in automated decision-making processes.

Additionally, **data privacy** and **cybersecurity** are critical considerations. As companies adopt AI-driven automation, they are also collecting and processing vast amounts of sensitive data. Ensuring that this data is protected and used ethically is essential to maintaining trust and safeguarding customer information.

To address these challenges, organizations are adopting **AI governance frameworks** that set clear guidelines for the ethical use of AI. These frameworks include regular audits, transparency measures, and data protection protocols to ensure that AI systems are fair, secure, and accountable.

Final Thoughts: The future of AI-driven automation is filled with potential. As technology continues to evolve, we can expect AI to play an even greater role in improving efficiency, driving innovation, and reshaping industries. From self-driving cars to AI-powered factories, the possibilities are endless.

However, as automation becomes more widespread, organizations must also focus on **reskilling** their workforce, addressing ethical concerns, and ensuring that AI is used responsibly. By doing so, we can harness the full potential of AI automation to build a more efficient, innovative, and inclusive future.

Looking Ahead : In Chapter 7, we will explore how AI is reshaping the way businesses interact with their customers. We'll discuss how AI-driven personalization, predictive analytics, and conversational interfaces are revolutionizing customer experiences, making interactions more intuitive, responsive, and tailored. By putting the customer at the center of AI applications, organizations can not only enhance satisfaction but also foster loyalty and drive growth in a competitive marketplace. Get ready to uncover the power of customer-centric AI and its impact on building stronger, more meaningful connections with customers.

7

Customer-Centric AI: Transforming Experiences

"AI makes experiences personal, turning data into deeper connections."

In today's digital world, customer experience is the new battlefield where businesses differentiate themselves. As companies compete to meet rising consumer expectations, **AI-driven customer experiences** have emerged as a critical tool for improving personalization, engagement, and satisfaction. In this chapter, we'll explore how AI is transforming customer experiences across industries, enhancing personalization, and creating deeper connections between brands and consumers.

The Shift to Customer-Centric AI

As digital transformation accelerates, businesses are focusing more than ever on delivering personalized, seamless customer experiences. Today's customers expect brands to know their preferences, anticipate their needs, and deliver tailored solutions at the right time. According to a **2025 PwC survey**, **76% of consumers** now say a personalized experience is a key factor in their purchasing decisions—up from 73% last year.

AI plays a pivotal role in helping companies meet these expectations. By analyzing vast amounts of customer data—from browsing history to purchase patterns—AI systems can predict customer preferences and deliver personalized recommendations, offers, and experiences in real time. **AI-driven personalization** is becoming a cornerstone of modern customer engagement strategies, enabling businesses to offer tailored experiences at scale.

Personalization at Scale: How AI Delivers Tailored Experiences

One of the most transformative aspects of AI is its ability to deliver **personalization at scale**. In the past, providing a personalized experience was a manual and time-consuming process that could only be done for a select few customers. Today, AI allows companies to personalize experiences for millions of customers simultaneously, without sacrificing quality.

For example, Netflix continues to fine-tune its recommendation engine. As of **2025**, internal data reveals that **over 85%** of streamed content is influenced by AI-powered suggestions. This level of personalization keeps viewers engaged and increases satisfaction by delivering content that resonates on an individual level.

In e-commerce, AI is helping retailers deliver hyper-personalized shopping experiences. Amazon reports that **AI-driven product recommendations now contribute to 38% of its total sales**, as of a **2024 study by Digital Commerce 360**. By analyzing customer behavior and preferences, AI helps create intuitive shopping journeys that drive both engagement and conversion.

AI and the Omnichannel Experience

Customers today interact with brands across multiple touchpoints—whether it's on a website, mobile app, social media, or in-store. These omnichannel experiences require consistency, and AI is crucial in ensuring that customers receive a seamless and personalized journey regardless of the platform they use.

AI-powered virtual assistants and chatbots are at the forefront of this transformation. According to **Gartner's 2024 CX Insights**, businesses using advanced AI chatbots have seen a **47% reduction in customer support costs**, alongside measurable improvements in customer satisfaction and resolution speed.

Brands like Sephora continue to lead by example. Its AI-driven chatbot now engages users across web, mobile, and social channels, offering product tips and customized beauty advice. In 2025, Sephora reported a **19% increase in conversion rates** through chatbot-assisted purchases—demonstrating the tangible value of consistent, intelligent customer engagement.

Predicting Customer Needs with AI

AI's predictive capabilities allow businesses to anticipate customer needs before they even arise, creating proactive and delightful customer experiences. By analyzing historical data, AI can predict future behavior and offer personalized solutions that meet the customer's needs at just the right moment.

In **retail**, this means AI can predict when a customer is likely to run out of a product and send a timely reminder or offer. **Walmart**, for example, uses AI algorithms to analyze customer purchasing patterns and recommend products that align with their preferences and buying habits. This predictive approach not only increases sales but also creates a more convenient shopping experience for the customer.

In **finance**, AI is being used to provide proactive financial advice. For example, **Bank of America's AI assistant, Erica**, helps customers manage their accounts by analyzing transaction data and suggesting ways to save money, avoid overdraft fees, or manage spending. **Erica** is now used by over **35 million users** as of 2025. According to a recent **internal report by Bank of America**, AI-powered proactive banking features have led to a **25% increase** in customer satisfaction scores.

Enhancing Customer Engagement Through AI

AI's ability to analyze customer behavior and preferences in real time allows businesses to engage with customers in more meaningful and relevant ways. This is particularly valuable in **marketing** and **advertising**, where AI-powered systems can deliver personalized content, offers, and ads that resonate with individual customers.

According to a **2024 McKinsey report**, companies that leverage AI-driven customer engagement strategies see **5-10% increases in revenue** while reducing churn. This is because AI enables businesses to engage customers at the right time with the right message, creating more personalized and targeted interactions that drive loyalty and repeat purchases.

Spotify is another standout example. Its AI continues to refine user experiences by crafting hyper-personalized playlists. In 2025, Spotify disclosed a **45% increase in user engagement and retention**, thanks to its ability to match listeners with music that fits their mood, history, and habits

AI and Emotional Intelligence in Customer Service

While AI excels at providing efficiency and personalization, it's also starting to develop **emotional intelligence**—the ability to understand and respond to human emotions. By analyzing sentiment in customer communications, AI systems can adjust their responses based on the customer's emotional state, improving the overall experience.

Emotion AI or **affective computing** is helping businesses provide more empathetic and human-like customer interactions. For example, if an AI-powered virtual assistant detects frustration in a customer's voice or language, it can escalate the issue to a human agent or offer a more empathetic response. While AI excels at providing efficiency and personalization, it's also starting to develop emotional intelligence—the ability to understand and respond to human emotions. By analyzing sentiment in customer communications, AI systems can adjust their responses based on the customer's emotional state, improving the overall experience.

Emotion AI, or affective computing, is gaining ground. A **2024 report by Forrester** found that businesses using emotion-aware AI in customer service saw a **15% boost in customer satisfaction**, driven by more empathetic and timely support.

In **contact centers**, real-time sentiment analysis is being used to coach agents during live interactions. AI tools now detect frustration or confusion in a customer's voice and recommend appropriate responses on the fly. This real-time support is helping agents build stronger, more human connections—one conversation at a time.

Challenges in AI-Driven Customer Experience

While AI has the potential to revolutionize customer experiences, it also presents challenges that businesses must address. One of the primary concerns is **data privacy**. AI systems rely on vast amounts of customer data to deliver personalized experiences, and companies must ensure that this data is collected, stored, and used in compliance with privacy regulations such as the **General Data Protection Regulation (GDPR)** and the **California Consumer Privacy Act (CCPA)**.

Another challenge is ensuring **fairness** in AI-driven decisions. AI systems can sometimes reinforce biases present in the data they are trained on, leading to unfair outcomes in areas like credit scoring, hiring, and product recommendations. Companies must invest in **bias mitigation strategies** and regularly audit their AI systems to ensure they are delivering fair and unbiased outcomes.

Best Practices for Implementing AI in Customer Experience

To fully realize the potential of AI in transforming customer experiences, businesses should adopt the following best practices:

1. **Data Transparency and Privacy**: Be transparent with customers about how their data is being used and ensure compliance with privacy regulations. Provide customers with control over their data and allow them to opt out of data collection if they choose.

2. **Bias Audits**: Regularly audit AI algorithms to identify and address biases. This can help ensure that AI systems deliver fair and equitable experiences for all customers.

3. **Human-AI Collaboration**: Use AI to augment human workers, not replace them. Human oversight is critical in ensuring that AI-driven customer experiences are empathetic, fair, and aligned with the company's values.

4. **Continuous Improvement**: AI systems should be regularly updated and fine-tuned to adapt to changing customer preferences and behaviors. Invest in ongoing research and development to ensure that AI remains a powerful tool for enhancing customer experience.

Final Thoughts: AI-driven customer experiences are rapidly evolving, and their impact on businesses will only grow in the coming years. As AI continues to improve personalization, predict customer needs, and enhance emotional intelligence, companies that embrace these technologies will be better positioned to build lasting relationships with their customers.

Looking Ahead: In the next chapter, we'll explore how building an AI-ready culture within organizations is essential for successfully implementing AI strategies. From leadership buy-in to employee training, creating a culture that embraces AI is key to unlocking its full potential.

8
Building an AI-Ready Culture

"An AI-powered future begins with a culture that embraces learning and collaboration."

As AI continues to reshape industries and revolutionize workflows, one thing has become clear: AI implementation is not just about technology; it's about people and culture. To fully realize the benefits of AI, organizations need to cultivate an **AI-ready culture**—one that fosters a digital-first mindset, encourages innovation, and empowers employees to embrace new technologies. In this chapter, we'll explore the steps organizations must take to build an AI-ready culture and the cultural shift required to successfully integrate AI into their operations.

The Importance of an AI-Ready Culture

Successfully integrating AI into an organization requires more than just adopting new technologies; it demands a significant **cultural shift**. AI doesn't just change the tools employees use—it transforms the way they work, make decisions, and collaborate. Without the right culture in place, AI initiatives are likely to face resistance, confusion, and inefficiencies.

According to a **2023 Deloitte survey, 60% of business leaders** identified cultural challenges as the primary obstacle to successful AI implementation. Building an AI-ready culture means preparing employees for the changes AI will bring, fostering an environment where innovation thrives, and ensuring that teams are aligned with the organization's AI strategy.

Cultivating a Digital-First Mindset

At the heart of an AI-ready culture is a **digital-first mindset**—an approach that prioritizes digital tools and technologies in every aspect of the organization's operations. This mindset encourages employees to think digitally, leveraging AI and other technologies to solve problems, enhance efficiency, and drive innovation.

To cultivate a digital-first mindset, organizations should:

- **Encourage Continuous Learning**: AI is a rapidly evolving field, and employees need to stay up to date with the latest developments. Organizations should invest in training programs, workshops, and certifications that help employees develop AI literacy and digital skills. According to **LinkedIn's 2024 Workplace Learning Report**, companies that prioritize continuous learning are **46% more likely** to successfully integrate AI into their operations.

- **Foster an Innovation-Driven Culture**: AI thrives in environments where experimentation and innovation are encouraged. Companies should create spaces where employees feel comfortable testing new ideas, exploring AI applications, and taking risks. **Google**, for example, promotes a culture of innovation by allowing employees to spend **20% of their work time** on projects outside of their core responsibilities, encouraging creativity and new AI-driven initiatives.

- **Lead by Example**: Leadership plays a crucial role in building an AI-ready culture. When leaders demonstrate a commitment to AI and digital transformation, employees are more likely to follow suit. According to a **2023 McKinsey report**, organizations with leaders who actively support AI adoption are **2.5 times more likely** to see successful AI outcomes.

Preparing the Workforce for AI Integration

For many employees, AI can seem intimidating, especially if they fear that automation may replace their jobs. To ease these concerns and prepare the workforce for AI integration, organizations must focus on **upskilling** and **reskilling** employees, empowering them to work alongside AI and leverage it as a tool to enhance their roles.

- **Upskilling for the AI Age**: Employees need to develop new skills to thrive in an AI-driven workplace. This includes not only technical skills like data analysis, machine learning, and programming but also **soft skills** such as critical thinking, adaptability, and emotional intelligence. According to a **2024 World Economic Forum report**, **50% of all employees** will need reskilling by 2025 to keep pace with AI and automation.

- **Collaboration Between Humans and AI**: One of the key aspects of an AI-ready culture is understanding that AI is not here to replace humans, but to **augment** their abilities. AI can handle repetitive tasks and data-heavy processes, freeing up employees to focus on strategic decision-making, creativity, and problem-solving. Organizations should promote a **collaborative mindset**, where employees view AI as a partner that enhances their productivity rather than a threat to their jobs.

- **Cross-Functional Teams**: AI integration often requires collaboration between technical and non-technical teams. **Cross-functional teams**—which bring together data scientists, AI engineers, and business leaders—are essential to ensure that AI initiatives align with business objectives. These teams can work together to identify areas where AI can add value, implement AI solutions, and ensure that AI-driven insights are used effectively across the organization.

Overcoming Resistance to Change

Resistance to change is one of the biggest barriers to building an AI-ready culture. Employees may be hesitant to adopt AI technologies due to fears of job displacement, lack of understanding, or skepticism about the benefits of AI. To overcome this resistance, organizations need to focus on **communication**, **transparency**, and **employee involvement**.

- **Communicate the Benefits of AI**: Clear communication is key to alleviating fears and building trust. Employees need to understand how AI will benefit not only the organization but also their individual roles. According to a **2023 survey by PwC**, employees who understood how AI would enhance their work were **38% more likely** to support AI adoption. Companies should provide regular updates on AI initiatives, highlight success stories, and demonstrate how AI is improving workflows, efficiency, and customer satisfaction.

- **Involve Employees in the AI Journey**: When employees are actively involved in AI initiatives, they are more likely to embrace the changes AI brings. Organizations should create opportunities for employees to participate in AI projects, whether through pilot programs, hackathons, or AI-focused innovation labs. **Unilever**, for example, launched an internal AI incubator where employees could propose and test AI-driven ideas, leading to greater engagement and support for AI across the company.

- **Address Job Displacement Concerns**: One of the most common fears employees have about AI is that it will lead to job loss. To address these concerns, companies must emphasize that AI is a tool for enhancing human roles, not replacing them. By focusing on **job transformation** rather than job elimination, organizations can reassure employees that AI will help them work smarter, not harder.

Creating a Culture of Data-Driven Decision Making

AI thrives in environments where data is valued and used to inform decision-making. Building an AI-ready culture means fostering a **data-driven mindset** across the organization, where decisions are based on insights derived from AI and analytics rather than intuition or gut feelings.

- **Democratizing Data Access**: For AI to be successful, employees across all levels of the organization need access to data. This requires creating systems and processes that allow employees to easily access and analyze data, whether they are data scientists, marketing professionals, or customer service representatives. **Microsoft**, for example, implemented a company-wide data platform that democratizes access to AI-driven insights, enabling teams across departments to make more informed decisions.

- **Empowering Employees with AI Tools**: Providing employees with AI-powered tools that simplify data analysis and decision-making is key to fostering a data-driven culture. **AI-powered dashboards**, **predictive analytics platforms**, and **automation tools** enable employees to analyze trends, forecast outcomes, and make data-backed decisions in real time. According to a **2023 survey by IBM**, organizations that empower employees with AI tools are **35% more likely** to make faster and more accurate business decisions.

- **Data Literacy Programs**: To build a culture where data-driven decision-making thrives, employees need to be data literate. This means understanding how to interpret data, recognize patterns, and draw actionable insights. Companies should invest in **data literacy programs** that help employees develop these skills, regardless of their role or department.

The Role of Leadership in Driving AI Culture

Leadership plays a central role in driving an AI-ready culture. Leaders set the tone for how AI is perceived and integrated into the organization. When leaders champion AI, employees are more likely to follow suit. **Transformational leadership**—where leaders inspire and empower employees to embrace change—has been shown to be particularly effective in fostering an AI-ready culture.

1. **Lead by Example**: Leaders should demonstrate their commitment to AI by using AI-driven tools, making data-backed decisions, and encouraging innovation. When leaders actively engage with AI, it sends a message to the rest of the organization that AI is a priority.

- **Set a Clear AI Vision**: Employees need to understand how AI fits into the organization's broader goals. Leaders should communicate a **clear AI vision**, outlining how AI will enhance the company's operations, drive innovation, and create value for customers. This vision should be reinforced through regular updates and success stories.

- **Encourage Experimentation**: AI is an evolving field, and organizations need to foster a culture of experimentation where employees feel empowered to test new ideas and applications. Leaders should support AI pilot projects, encourage employees to take calculated risks, and celebrate both successes and learnings.

Final Thoughts: Building an AI-ready culture is an ongoing process that requires commitment, collaboration, and a willingness to adapt. As AI becomes more deeply embedded in business operations, organizations that prioritize culture will be better positioned to succeed in the AI age. By fostering a digital-first mindset, preparing employees for the future of work, and encouraging data-driven decision-making, companies can unlock the full potential of AI and drive long-term growth.

Looking Ahead: In the next chapter, we'll explore how AI is converging with other emerging technologies to accelerate digital transformation and create new opportunities for innovation.

9
The Convergence of AI with Emerging Technologies

"The true power of AI emerges when it converges with the technologies of tomorrow."

As artificial intelligence (AI) continues to evolve, its true transformative power is being realized when combined with other emerging technologies. AI is no longer operating in isolation—it is intersecting with innovations like the **Internet of Things (IoT)**, **blockchain**, **5G**, and **edge computing** to create new solutions that are driving the next wave of digital transformation. In this chapter, we'll explore how the convergence of AI with these technologies is reshaping industries and unlocking unprecedented opportunities for efficiency, security, and innovation.

AI and IoT: The Smart Connection

The **Internet of Things (IoT)** has become one of the most powerful platforms for collecting data from physical environments—whether it's in smart cities, factories, or homes. However, IoT by itself only collects data; AI is what enables systems to analyze and act on that data in real time. By combining AI with IoT, businesses can transform raw data into actionable insights, allowing machines and devices to operate more intelligently.

According to a **2024 report by IDC**, there will be over **30 billion connected IoT devices** globally by 2025. This explosion of IoT devices—ranging from sensors in industrial machines to smart thermostats in homes—is generating massive amounts of data that can be analyzed by AI to optimize processes, predict maintenance needs, and enhance user experiences.

In **smart cities**, AI and IoT are working together to manage traffic flows, monitor energy usage, and even improve public safety. For example, **Barcelona** uses AI and IoT to manage its water supply system, reducing water waste by **25%** while ensuring a steady and reliable supply to its residents. Similarly, in **manufacturing**,

AI-powered IoT systems are transforming **Industry 4.0**, enabling predictive maintenance and reducing downtime by analyzing real-time data from sensors on production lines.

AI and Blockchain: Enhancing Security and Transparency

While AI excels at processing and analyzing data, **blockchain** offers a decentralized and secure way to store that data. The convergence of AI and blockchain provides a powerful combination that enhances both security and transparency, especially in industries that rely on trust, such as finance, healthcare, and supply chain management.

Blockchain's decentralized ledger ensures that data is immutable—meaning it cannot be altered once it's recorded. This is particularly valuable in AI applications where data integrity is critical. For instance, in **supply chains**, AI can analyze data from IoT sensors tracking products as they move through the supply chain, while blockchain ensures that the data is accurate and verifiable at every step. According to a **2023 World Economic Forum report**, AI and blockchain together can reduce inefficiencies and fraud in global supply chains by **50%**.

In **finance**, AI algorithms are being used to analyze transaction data and detect fraudulent activity, while blockchain secures those transactions on a decentralized ledger, making them tamper-proof. Companies like **JP Morgan** have implemented AI-blockchain systems to improve the security of their digital payment platforms, reducing fraud-related losses by **27%** in 2023.

AI and 5G: Unlocking Real-Time Intelligence

The rollout of **5G networks** is unlocking new possibilities for AI by enabling real-time data processing and communication at lightning-fast speeds. With **speeds up to 100 times faster than 4G**, 5G allows AI to process vast amounts of data instantly, making it ideal for applications that require real-time responses, such as autonomous vehicles, smart cities, and remote healthcare.

According to **Ericsson's 2024 Mobility Report**, 5G **coverage** will reach **75% of the global population** by 2026, and its combination with AI will drive innovations across multiple sectors. One of the most notable applications is in **autonomous vehicles**. AI-powered self-driving cars rely on real-time data from sensors, cameras, and GPS to navigate roads, avoid obstacles, and make split-second decisions. 5G's ultra-low latency enables these vehicles to communicate with other cars and infrastructure in real time, making them safer and more efficient.

In **healthcare**, 5G and AI are enabling remote surgeries and real-time diagnostics. AI-powered systems can analyze medical images, monitor patient vitals, and even assist in surgical procedures, all while a doctor oversees the operation remotely. A **2023 study by the U.S. Department of Health and Human Services** estimated that 5G-enabled AI could reduce the time it takes to diagnose and treat patients by **15-20%**, leading to better patient outcomes.

AI and Edge Computing: Bringing Intelligence to the Edge

With the rise of IoT and connected devices, there is a growing need to process data closer to where it's generated—at the "edge" of the network—rather than relying on distant cloud servers. **Edge computing** brings data processing closer to the source, reducing latency, improving response times, and increasing efficiency. When combined with AI, edge computing enables faster decision-making, especially in environments where real-time data processing is critical.

In **retail**, AI-powered edge computing is transforming the shopping experience. Smart cameras and sensors installed in stores can analyze customer behavior in real time, adjusting digital displays, offering personalized promotions, and optimizing store layouts to drive sales. **Walmart**, for example, uses edge computing and AI to manage its inventory in real time, reducing stockouts and improving customer satisfaction.

In **agriculture**, AI-powered drones and edge computing systems are helping farmers monitor crops, predict weather conditions, and optimize water usage. By processing data locally—whether it's from soil sensors or satellite images—farmers can make immediate decisions that improve crop yields and reduce resource waste. A **2023 report by the United Nations** estimated that AI and edge computing could increase global agricultural productivity by **25-30%** while reducing water usage by **15-20%**.

The Future of AI Convergence

The convergence of AI with IoT, blockchain, 5G, and edge computing is just the beginning. These technologies are rapidly evolving, and their combined impact will only grow in the coming years. According to a **2024 Accenture report, 80% of business leaders** believe that the convergence of these technologies will be the key driver of innovation over the next decade.

One exciting area of future convergence is the development of **smart grids**—energy systems that combine AI, IoT, and blockchain to optimize energy distribution, reduce waste, and increase the use of renewable energy. AI algorithms can predict energy demand and supply, while IoT sensors monitor energy usage in real time. Blockchain ensures that energy transactions between producers and consumers are transparent and secure. According to a **2023 Bloomberg NEF report**, smart grids could reduce energy costs by **15-20%** for consumers while promoting the adoption of green energy sources.

In **healthcare**, the convergence of AI, 5G, and edge computing will enable the development of **smart hospitals**, where real-time patient monitoring, AI-driven diagnostics, and remote surgeries become the norm. These technologies will not only improve patient outcomes but also make healthcare more accessible, especially in rural areas where access to medical specialists is limited.

Challenges of AI Convergence

While the convergence of AI with emerging technologies presents exciting opportunities, it also introduces new challenges. One of the primary concerns is **data privacy**. With IoT devices collecting vast amounts of personal data and AI analyzing that data in real time, ensuring that privacy regulations like the **General Data Protection Regulation (GDPR)** and the **California Consumer Privacy Act (CCPA)** are followed is critical.

Additionally, the convergence of AI with blockchain and 5G requires **interoperability**—the ability of different systems and devices to communicate and work together seamlessly. As these technologies evolve, businesses must invest in developing standards and protocols that ensure compatibility across platforms.

Final Thoughts: The convergence of AI with IoT, blockchain, 5G, and edge computing is unlocking a new era of innovation and efficiency. As these technologies continue to mature, they will revolutionize industries ranging from healthcare and agriculture to finance and manufacturing. Businesses that embrace this convergence will be better positioned to drive growth, enhance customer experiences, and lead the next wave of digital transformation.

Looking Ahead: In the next chapter, we will dive into the vital role of AI in promoting sustainability and addressing the environmental challenges of our digital era. We'll explore how Green AI initiatives are helping businesses reduce their carbon footprint, optimize resource usage, and drive eco-friendly innovations. By embracing sustainable AI practices, organizations can balance technological advancement with environmental stewardship, ensuring that digital transformation contributes positively to our planet. Join us as we uncover how AI can be a force for good, fostering a greener, more sustainable future.

10
Sustainability in the Digital Age: Embracing Green AI

"The future of AI must not only be intelligent but sustainable."

As the world becomes increasingly digital, concerns about the environmental impact of technology are rising. From energy-intensive data centers to the growing problem of **e-waste**, the tech industry faces significant challenges in terms of sustainability. In response, a new movement is emerging—**Green AI**, an approach to developing and using artificial intelligence in ways that prioritize energy efficiency, reduce carbon footprints, and promote sustainability. In this chapter, we'll explore how Green AI is helping to address some of the biggest environmental challenges of the digital age and how businesses can embrace AI as a force for good.

The Environmental Cost of AI

While AI offers immense benefits, it also comes with a significant environmental cost. Training large AI models, particularly those that rely on **deep learning**, requires enormous amounts of computational power, leading to high energy consumption. According to a **2023 study by the University of Massachusetts**, training a single deep learning model can emit as much carbon dioxide as **five cars over their entire lifetimes**. As AI adoption continues to grow, so does its carbon footprint.

In addition to the energy consumed by training AI models, the infrastructure that supports AI—such as data centers—also contributes to environmental degradation. Data centers, which house the servers and networks that power AI systems, account for approximately **1% of global electricity use** as of 2024. This figure is expected to rise as more companies adopt AI-driven solutions and store vast amounts of data in the cloud.

Recognizing these environmental concerns, researchers, tech companies, and policymakers are increasingly focused on developing AI in ways that minimize its environmental impact. This has given rise to the concept of **Green AI**—an approach to AI development that prioritizes sustainability and seeks to reduce the environmental costs associated with AI technologies.

What is Green AI?

Green AI refers to the development and deployment of AI systems that are designed to be energy-efficient and environmentally friendly. The goal of Green AI is to reduce the carbon emissions associated with AI while still enabling innovation and technological progress. This can be achieved through a variety of strategies, such as optimizing algorithms for energy efficiency, using renewable energy to power data centers, and promoting sustainable hardware development.

Several leading tech companies have committed to embracing Green AI as part of their broader sustainability goals. For example, **Google** has pledged to operate its data centers on **100% renewable energy** by 2030, and **Microsoft** has committed to becoming **carbon negative** by 2030, meaning it will remove more carbon from the atmosphere than it emits.

AI for Energy Efficiency

One of the most significant ways that AI can contribute to sustainability is by improving **energy efficiency** across industries. AI algorithms can analyze energy usage data in real time, identifying inefficiencies and optimizing systems to reduce waste.

This is particularly important in energy-intensive industries like manufacturing, transportation, and construction.

For example, in **smart buildings**, AI-powered systems can monitor energy usage and automatically adjust lighting, heating, and cooling systems to reduce energy consumption. By using data from IoT sensors and AI algorithms, smart buildings can reduce energy use by **30-40%**, according to a **2024 report by the International Energy Agency (IEA)**. Similarly, AI is being used to optimize **logistics and transportation**, where route planning algorithms can reduce fuel consumption and emissions by predicting the most efficient routes for delivery trucks and fleets.

In **data centers**, which are responsible for powering the cloud infrastructure that supports AI, AI-driven energy management systems can significantly reduce energy consumption. **Google's DeepMind** has used AI to optimize the cooling systems in its data centers, reducing energy use by **30%** and cutting its overall energy costs by **15%**. This type of AI-driven efficiency is crucial for reducing the environmental impact of the tech industry as data demands continue to grow.

Tackling E-Waste with AI

Another major environmental challenge in the digital age is **e-waste**—the disposal of electronic devices such as smartphones, computers, and servers. In 2023, the world generated over **57.4 million metric tons** of e-waste, according to the **Global E-Waste Monitor**, and this figure is expected to continue rising as more devices are produced and discarded. E-waste not only contributes to landfill pollution but also releases hazardous materials such as lead and mercury into the environment.

AI is helping to address the growing problem of e-waste by improving **recycling processes** and enabling more efficient use of materials. For example, AI-powered robotics systems are being used to automate the sorting of e-waste, identifying valuable materials such as gold, copper, and aluminum that can be extracted and reused. This technology is improving the efficiency of recycling facilities and reducing the amount of e-waste that ends up in landfills.

In addition to recycling, AI is also being used to promote the **circular economy**, where products are designed to be reused, repaired, and recycled rather than disposed of. For example, AI algorithms can analyze data from IoT sensors embedded in electronic devices to predict when they will need maintenance or replacement. This enables companies to extend the lifespan of their products, reducing the need for new devices and minimizing e-waste.

AI and Renewable Energy

AI is playing a key role in accelerating the adoption of **renewable energy** sources such as wind, solar, and hydroelectric power. By using AI to analyze weather patterns, predict energy generation, and manage energy storage, companies are able to integrate renewable energy more effectively into the grid.

For example, **DeepMind** has developed AI models that predict the output of **wind farms** 36 hours in advance, allowing energy providers to better plan and allocate resources. This has increased the efficiency of wind energy by **20%**, according to a **2023 DeepMind report**. Similarly, AI is being used to optimize

solar energy production by analyzing weather data and adjusting the positioning of solar panels to capture the maximum amount of sunlight.

In addition to optimizing energy production, AI is helping to manage **energy storage** solutions, such as batteries and pumped hydro storage, which are essential for ensuring a reliable supply of renewable energy. AI algorithms can predict when energy demand will peak and adjust storage levels accordingly, reducing the need for fossil fuel-based backup power.

Green AI in Tech Development

As AI becomes more integrated into the development of new technologies, it is crucial that sustainability remains a priority. Companies are beginning to adopt **sustainable design principles** when developing AI-driven products, focusing on reducing energy consumption, minimizing material waste, and promoting the use of eco-friendly materials.

For example, the development of **energy-efficient hardware**—such as AI chips that require less power to operate—can significantly reduce the environmental impact of AI systems. According to a **2023 report by the Semiconductor Industry Association**, next-generation AI chips are expected to consume **10-20% less energy** than current models, making them a more sustainable option for data centers and AI applications.

In addition to hardware, AI is being used to **optimize software** for energy efficiency. AI-driven code optimization tools can analyze software applications and suggest changes that reduce their energy consumption, making them more sustainable to run on servers and devices.

Best Practices for Embracing Green AI

To fully embrace Green AI and promote sustainability in the digital age, businesses should adopt the following best practices:

1. **Optimize AI Algorithms for Energy Efficiency**: Ensure that AI algorithms are designed to minimize energy consumption by using techniques such as model compression, pruning, and quantization. These techniques reduce the computational resources needed to run AI models, making them more energy-efficient.

2. **Use Renewable Energy to Power AI Infrastructure**: Data centers and AI-powered systems should be powered by renewable energy sources such as wind, solar, and hydroelectric power. Companies should commit to reducing their reliance on fossil fuels and invest in renewable energy solutions for their operations.

3. **Promote the Circular Economy**: Design AI-driven products with sustainability in mind, focusing on reuse, repair, and recycling. By extending the lifespan of products and reducing material waste, companies can minimize the environmental impact of their technologies.

4. **Invest in AI for Sustainability**: Encourage innovation by investing in AI-driven solutions that address environmental challenges, such as energy management, waste reduction, and renewable energy optimization. By focusing on sustainability, businesses can create value while reducing their carbon footprint.

Final Thoughts: In the digital age, sustainability is essential. Green AI offers a way to blend innovation with environmental responsibility, driving positive change through efficient, eco-friendly practices. By adopting Green AI, we can make a lasting impact and transform digital advancements into catalysts for a more sustainable future.

Looking Ahead: As AI continues to evolve, its role in promoting sustainability will become increasingly important. By embracing Green AI and adopting sustainable practices, businesses can not only reduce their environmental impact but also contribute to a more sustainable future for the planet. In the next chapter, we'll explore further on Green AI and deep dive into how we can enable a greener digital transformation.

11
Green AI: Enabling a Greener Digital Transformation

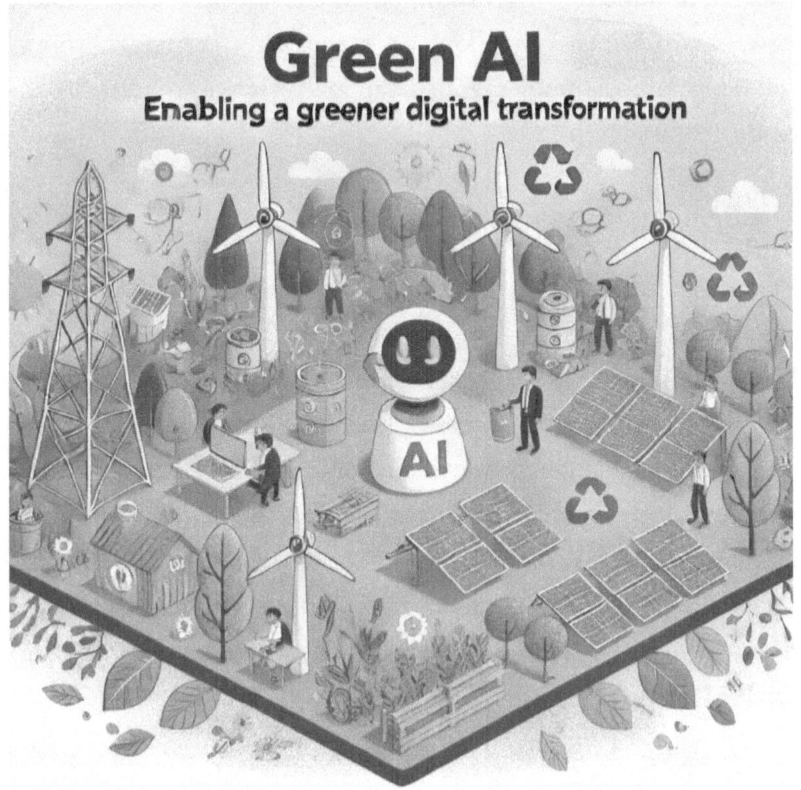

"True innovation balances technological progress with environmental responsibility."

As AI continues to push the boundaries of innovation, it also brings with it the responsibility to ensure that its development and deployment do not come at the expense of the environment. While AI has the potential to revolutionize industries, it is also an energy-intensive technology that contributes to rising carbon emissions. In response, businesses and organizations are embracing **Green AI**—an approach that balances technological advancement with environmental responsibility. In this chapter, we'll explore how organizations can adopt AI responsibly, minimize energy consumption, and implement sustainable practices to mitigate the environmental impact of AI.

The Environmental Impact of AI Innovation

The benefits of AI are clear: it enables automation, drives innovation, and helps organizations unlock new efficiencies. However, AI models—especially **large-scale neural networks**—are extremely resource-intensive. Training AI models, such as those used for natural language processing or image recognition, requires substantial computational power, which consumes significant amounts of energy. According to a **2023 study by MIT**, training a single large AI model can emit over **284 metric tons of carbon dioxide**—equivalent to the emissions of **five cars over their entire lifetimes**.

Moreover, AI systems rely on **data centers**, which house the servers, storage systems, and networking infrastructure necessary to support AI-driven technologies. These data centers consume vast amounts of electricity, much of which is still generated by non-renewable sources like coal and natural gas. As more organizations adopt AI, the energy demand from these data centers will only increase. The **International Energy Agency (IEA)** predicts that by 2025, data centers could account for **3.2% of global electricity demand**.

To address these concerns, organizations must take a proactive approach to adopting Green AI, ensuring that AI innovation aligns with sustainability goals and minimizes environmental harm.

Key Strategies for Adopting Green AI

Adopting Green AI is not about sacrificing innovation for sustainability. Instead, it's about finding ways to balance the two—driving AI advancements while reducing the environmental impact of AI technologies. Here are key strategies that organizations can adopt to ensure their AI initiatives are both cutting-edge and environmentally responsible:

- **Optimizing AI Algorithms for Energy Efficiency** AI developers can take steps to ensure that their algorithms are optimized for energy efficiency. This involves using techniques such as **model pruning, quantization**, and **knowledge distillation** to reduce the computational resources required to train and run AI models. These techniques allow AI systems to maintain high performance while using fewer resources.

  For example, **model pruning** involves removing unnecessary parameters from a neural network, reducing the size of the model and thus lowering the computational power needed to train and deploy it. Similarly, **quantization** reduces the precision of calculations in a model, allowing it to operate more efficiently without sacrificing accuracy.

A **2024 report by Google's AI Research team** found that by optimizing AI models for energy efficiency, organizations can reduce energy consumption by **15-25%** without compromising performance. As AI continues to scale, these optimization techniques will play a critical role in mitigating its environmental impact.

- **Leveraging Renewable Energy for AI Infrastructure** One of the most effective ways to reduce the carbon footprint of AI is by powering data centers and AI infrastructure with **renewable energy**. Companies like **Microsoft**, **Google**, and **Amazon** are already investing in renewable energy sources to power their AI-driven operations. For example, **Google** has committed to running its data centers on **100% carbon-free energy** by 2030, while **Microsoft** aims to be **carbon negative** by the same year.

  Transitioning to renewable energy not only reduces the environmental impact of AI but also supports broader sustainability goals. By investing in wind, solar, and hydroelectric power, organizations can reduce their reliance on fossil fuels and lower their overall emissions. According to a **2023 report by the U.S. Environmental Protection Agency (EPA)**, using renewable energy to power data centers can reduce carbon emissions by **50-60%** compared to traditional energy sources.

- **Using AI to Improve Operational Sustainability** AI itself can be a powerful tool for improving sustainability within organizations. AI algorithms can analyze data on energy usage, resource consumption, and operational efficiency to identify areas where businesses can reduce their environmental impact. By using AI to optimize processes, organizations can reduce waste, improve resource allocation, and minimize energy consumption.

For example, **AI-powered energy management systems** can monitor real-time data from IoT sensors to automatically adjust heating, cooling, and lighting systems in buildings, reducing energy consumption by **30-40%**. Similarly, **AI-driven supply chain optimization** can help businesses reduce transportation emissions by predicting demand and optimizing delivery routes, reducing fuel consumption and lowering carbon emissions.

In **manufacturing**, AI is being used to reduce material waste and improve production efficiency. AI algorithms can predict equipment failures, allowing manufacturers to perform maintenance before issues arise and reducing the need for replacement parts and energy-intensive repairs. According to a **2024 report by McKinsey**, companies that use AI to optimize their supply chains and operations can reduce their carbon footprint by up to **15%**.

- **Extending the Lifecycle of AI-Driven Products**
Sustainability isn't just about reducing emissions during the development and deployment of AI models—it's also about designing products and systems that have a longer lifecycle. By extending the lifespan of AI-driven technologies, organizations can reduce the frequency of hardware replacements, minimize e-waste, and reduce the energy required to produce new devices.

Organizations can embrace a **circular economy** approach, where AI-driven products are designed to be repaired, reused, and recycled rather than discarded. For example, AI-powered predictive maintenance systems can extend the lifespan of industrial equipment by detecting wear and tear before breakdowns occur. This reduces the need for replacements and lowers the environmental cost associated with manufacturing new equipment.

Additionally, tech companies are developing **energy-efficient AI hardware**, such as AI chips that consume less power while delivering high performance. These chips, designed with sustainability in mind, can be used in a variety of devices—from smartphones to autonomous vehicles—reducing the overall energy consumption of AI-powered products.

Balancing Innovation with Environmental Responsibility

While it's clear that AI has the potential to drive significant innovation, organizations must remain vigilant about the environmental impact of their AI initiatives. Striking a balance between technological advancement and environmental responsibility requires a concerted effort from both developers and decision-makers.

One of the primary ways to ensure responsible AI adoption is to implement **AI governance frameworks** that include sustainability as a key consideration. These frameworks should outline best practices for minimizing energy consumption, reducing emissions, and promoting transparency in AI development. For example, organizations can conduct **AI energy audits** to assess the environmental impact of their AI models and infrastructure, and set targets for reducing their carbon footprint.

In addition, organizations should foster a culture of **sustainability-focused innovation**, encouraging employees to consider the environmental implications of their work. This can be achieved by incorporating sustainability goals into product development roadmaps and performance metrics, ensuring that environmental responsibility is at the forefront of AI initiatives.

The Role of Policy and Regulation

Governments and regulatory bodies also play a critical role in promoting Green AI and ensuring that the tech industry operates in an environmentally responsible manner. In recent years, policymakers have introduced regulations aimed at reducing the carbon emissions of data centers and encouraging the use of renewable energy in tech development.

For example, the **European Union's Green Deal** includes provisions to make data centers climate neutral by 2030, requiring companies to adopt sustainable practices and improve energy efficiency. Similarly, the **United States Clean Energy Standard** incentivizes companies to reduce emissions by offering tax credits for the use of renewable energy in data centers and cloud computing infrastructure.

As governments continue to prioritize climate action, it's likely that additional regulations will be introduced to ensure that AI development aligns with sustainability goals. Businesses that proactively adopt Green AI practices will not only comply with regulations but also position themselves as leaders in the push for environmentally responsible innovation.

Final Thoughts: Green AI is more than just a technological trend—it's a pathway to a sustainable digital future. By prioritizing energy efficiency and reducing environmental impacts, Green AI empowers businesses to innovate responsibly. Embracing Green AI not only supports digital transformation but also ensures that progress is aligned with the planet's long-term well-being

Looking Ahead: As we delve into the role of sustainability in digital transformation, we'll explore how integrating eco-friendly practices into AI initiatives can create enduring value. In the next chapter, we'll examine the strategies businesses can employ to ensure that their digital transformation efforts contribute to long-term environmental stewardship, driving innovation while protecting the planet for future generations.

12
Sustainability and Digital Transformation for Long-Term Impact

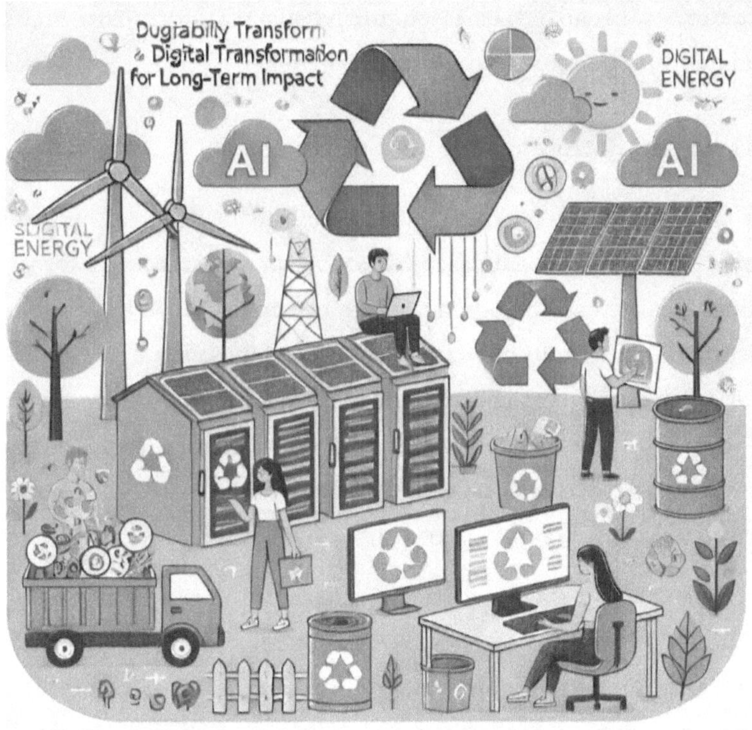

"The greatest transformations are those that benefit both businesses and the planet."

As businesses and governments around the world embark on their digital transformation journeys, the imperative to ensure that these advancements contribute to long-term **sustainability** has never been greater. **Artificial intelligence (AI)** is not just a tool for enhancing efficiency and driving innovation; it has the potential to be a powerful force for promoting **global sustainability**. From optimizing **supply chains** to fostering **eco-friendly innovation**, AI can help organizations minimize their environmental footprint while creating sustainable, long-term value. In this chapter, we'll explore how AI can be harnessed to drive sustainable transformation and deliver a positive impact on the planet.

AI's Role in Promoting Global Sustainability

As environmental concerns such as **climate change**, **resource depletion**, and **biodiversity loss** become increasingly urgent, businesses must recognize their responsibility to promote sustainability through technology. AI offers unique capabilities that can help address these challenges. By analyzing vast amounts of data, AI can uncover insights that enable organizations to **optimize energy usage**, **reduce waste**, and adopt more sustainable business practices.

AI is already playing a critical role in promoting sustainability in industries such as **energy, agriculture**, and **transportation**. For example, **renewable energy companies** are using AI to forecast energy demand and improve the efficiency of energy grids, while **agriculture** businesses are leveraging AI-driven technologies to optimize water usage and increase crop yields sustainably. According to a **2023 report by PwC**, AI technologies could reduce global greenhouse gas emissions by **4%** by 2030, while also creating new opportunities for innovation and growth in sustainable industries.

Sustainable Supply Chains Powered by AI

Supply chains are the backbone of the global economy, but they are also responsible for a significant portion of the world's carbon emissions. The good news is that AI can help companies **green their supply chains** by optimizing logistics, reducing waste, and minimizing energy consumption. By analyzing data from every stage of the supply chain—from raw materials to distribution—AI can identify inefficiencies and recommend more sustainable practices.

One of the key benefits of AI in supply chains is its ability to enable **predictive analytics**. AI can predict **demand fluctuations**, allowing businesses to optimize production levels and reduce overproduction. This leads to less wasted inventory, lower energy consumption, and a more efficient allocation of resources. AI-powered **inventory management** systems can also track stock levels in real time and optimize deliveries to reduce unnecessary transportation, cutting fuel consumption and emissions.

Additionally, AI can enhance **traceability** within supply chains, allowing businesses to track the environmental impact of their products from sourcing to distribution. This transparency enables companies to make more informed decisions about suppliers, materials, and processes, ensuring that their operations align with their sustainability goals.

Example of Success: Unilever's AI-Powered Supply Chain
Unilever, one of the world's largest consumer goods companies, has

used AI to create a more sustainable and efficient supply chain. By leveraging AI-powered **demand forecasting** tools, Unilever has reduced food waste, optimized production levels, and minimized excess inventory. Additionally, Unilever uses AI to monitor the environmental impact of its suppliers, ensuring that sustainability is embedded across its entire value chain. The company's efforts have resulted in a **30% reduction in CO2 emissions** across its global supply chain.

AI-Driven Innovations for Circular Economy

The transition to a **circular economy**—where products and materials are reused, repaired, and recycled rather than discarded—represents one of the most promising pathways for sustainable growth. AI is at the heart of this transition, enabling businesses to design products with **longevity** and **resource efficiency** in mind. By incorporating AI-driven insights into product development, companies can reduce waste, lower costs, and contribute to a more sustainable economy.

For instance, AI can analyze data on product usage, repair patterns, and customer feedback to inform the design of products that are easier to repair and recycle. This helps extend the lifecycle of products and reduces the need for new materials. AI-powered **recycling systems** can also improve the efficiency of waste sorting and material recovery, ensuring that valuable resources are reclaimed rather than sent to landfills.

AI's ability to optimize the use of resources also extends to industries like **construction** and **manufacturing**, where AI-powered systems can reduce material waste by recommending more efficient production methods. For example, AI algorithms can analyze construction blueprints to identify opportunities for reducing material usage or minimizing energy consumption during the building process.

Example of Success: **HP's Sustainable Design with AI** HP is a pioneer in leveraging AI to support the circular economy. The company has developed AI-powered tools that optimize the design of its products for **remanufacturing**, **recycling**, and **reuse**. By using AI to analyze the materials used in its products, HP has been able to increase the recyclability of its printers and reduce the overall environmental impact of its manufacturing processes. HP has also implemented AI-driven recycling systems that automatically sort and recover valuable materials from used electronics.

AI and Renewable Energy Optimization

One of the most critical areas where AI can drive sustainability is in the **renewable energy sector**. As the world transitions to cleaner energy sources such as wind, solar, and hydroelectric power, AI is playing a key role in making these sources more reliable and efficient.

AI-powered **energy management systems** use predictive analytics to forecast energy demand and optimize the integration of renewable energy into the grid. For example, AI can predict fluctuations in **solar energy production** based on weather patterns and adjust energy distribution accordingly. This helps utilities balance energy supply and demand, reducing reliance on fossil fuels during periods of high demand.

AI is also being used to optimize the performance of **wind turbines** and **solar panels**. By analyzing data from sensors installed on renewable energy infrastructure, AI can detect performance issues and recommend maintenance before equipment failures occur. This proactive approach to maintenance reduces downtime, improves energy output, and extends the lifespan of renewable energy infrastructure.

Example of Success: **Google's Use of AI for Renewable Energy** Google has been a leader in using AI to optimize the efficiency of its renewable energy operations. The company's **DeepMind AI** is used to predict the output of its wind farms up to 36 hours in advance, allowing Google to better plan and allocate energy resources. By using AI to improve wind energy forecasting, Google has increased the efficiency of its wind farms by **20%** and reduced its reliance on non-renewable energy sources.

AI's Role in Climate Resilience and Conservation

Beyond optimizing supply chains and energy use, AI is also being used to address the broader environmental challenges posed by **climate change** and **biodiversity loss**. AI-powered tools are helping scientists monitor and protect ecosystems, predict the impact of climate events, and support conservation efforts.

For example, AI-driven **remote sensing** technologies are being used to monitor deforestation, track wildlife populations, and assess the health of ecosystems. AI algorithms can analyze satellite imagery to detect illegal logging or poaching activities in real time, allowing conservationists to take swift action to protect endangered species and habitats.

In the realm of **climate resilience**, AI is being used to predict the impact of extreme weather events such as hurricanes, floods, and wildfires. These predictions enable governments and organizations to take proactive measures to mitigate damage and protect vulnerable communities.

Example of Success: **Microsoft's AI for Earth Initiative**
Microsoft's **AI for Earth** initiative uses AI technologies to tackle global environmental challenges, including climate change, conservation, and biodiversity loss. The initiative provides AI tools and resources to scientists, researchers, and environmental organizations working on sustainability projects. For example, Microsoft has partnered with **The Nature Conservancy** to use AI to analyze satellite data and monitor coral reef health. The project helps conservationists identify areas of coral degradation and develop strategies to protect and restore these vital ecosystems.

Best Practices for AI-Driven Sustainability

To fully harness the power of AI for sustainability, businesses must adopt best practices that ensure their digital transformation efforts are aligned with environmental goals. Here are some key strategies for promoting sustainability through AI:

1. **Integrate Sustainability into AI Development**: Sustainability should be a core consideration in every stage of AI development. This includes designing AI systems that optimize energy usage, reduce waste, and promote eco-friendly practices.

2. **Leverage AI for Resource Efficiency**: Businesses should use AI to monitor and optimize resource usage across their

operations. This includes using AI-powered systems to track energy consumption, minimize waste, and reduce emissions in real time.

3. **Collaborate for Greater Impact**: Sustainability is a global challenge, and no single organization can solve it alone. Businesses should collaborate with governments, NGOs, and other stakeholders to develop AI-driven solutions that address pressing environmental issues.

4. **Invest in Sustainable Innovation**: Companies should invest in AI-driven technologies that promote the circular economy, improve supply chain transparency, and enable renewable energy adoption. These innovations not only drive sustainability but also create long-term business value.

Final Thoughts: Sustainability is no longer just an option; it's a necessity for lasting digital transformation. As organizations embrace AI-driven technologies, they must align innovation with long-term environmental goals. By embedding sustainable practices into digital strategies, businesses can drive meaningful impact, reduce their carbon footprint, and set a positive example for future generations. Sustainability and digital transformation go hand in hand, paving the way for a resilient and responsible future.

Looking Ahead: AI-driven manipulation, fake news, and deepfakes represent a serious challenge to societal harmony, but with the right tools, policies, and public awareness, we can mitigate their impact. As AI continues to evolve, so too must our approaches to ensuring that it is used responsibly and ethically. In the next chapter, we'll discuss the steps society must take to build trust in AI, promote transparency, and harness its potential for good while mitigating the risks.

13
AI's Dark Power: Manipulating Minds

"Unchecked power in AI can create illusions—truth must remain the compass."

As artificial intelligence (AI) continues to transform industries and revolutionize the way we live, it has also introduced new threats to society. While AI offers tremendous opportunities for innovation, it has become a powerful tool for spreading **fake news**, creating **deepfakes**, and manipulating information—threatening the very fabric of trust and truth in modern society. In this chapter, we'll explore the darker side of AI, its potential to disrupt societal harmony, and the ways individuals, businesses, and governments can combat these challenges.

The Rise of AI-Driven Manipulation

AI's ability to process vast amounts of data, analyze human behavior, and generate realistic content has made it a potent tool for **manipulation**. With AI, malicious actors can create hyper-personalized content aimed at deceiving individuals, influencing their beliefs, and even inciting conflict. AI algorithms can quickly identify individuals' preferences, biases, and vulnerabilities, enabling the creation of tailored disinformation campaigns that are far more effective than traditional methods of manipulation.

One of the most concerning applications of AI-driven manipulation is in the spread of **fake news**. Fake news refers to the deliberate dissemination of false or misleading information with the intent to deceive or mislead the public. AI has made it easier to create fake news at scale, using natural language generation models to craft realistic-sounding articles, posts, and messages that appear credible.

According to a **2023 Pew Research Center report**, **64% of Americans** say that fake news causes confusion about the basic facts of current events. The rise of AI-generated fake news has exacerbated this problem, as AI can produce and spread disinformation faster than humans can fact-check it. The consequences of this are far-reaching, from influencing elections to eroding trust in public institutions and the media.

Deepfakes: The Threat of Digital Deception

Deepfakes represent another troubling application of AI. Deepfakes are hyper-realistic digital forgeries created by AI, in which a person's face, voice, or likeness is altered to create false yet believable audio or video content. These manipulations are so convincing that it can be nearly impossible for the average person to tell whether a video or audio clip is real or fake.

Deepfakes have been used for a variety of malicious purposes, from spreading false information about public figures to committing fraud. One of the most alarming uses of deepfakes is in **political disinformation** campaigns, where AI-generated videos of politicians making inflammatory or controversial statements are circulated to undermine public trust in elections and institutions. For example, during a 2023 election in Eastern Europe, a deepfake video of a political leader was released just days before voting, depicting the leader making damaging statements that were never actually said. The video went viral before it could be debunked, influencing public opinion and creating confusion among voters.

The **cybersecurity** implications of deepfakes are equally concerning. Criminals have used AI-generated deepfakes to impersonate executives and authorize fraudulent transactions. In one high-profile case in 2023, cybercriminals used an AI-generated deepfake of a CEO's voice to trick a financial institution into transferring millions of dollars to a fraudulent account—a scheme known as **voice phishing**.

According to a **2024 report by Sensity AI**, the number of deepfake videos circulating online has increased by **900%** since 2021, with political and corporate espionage, cybercrime, and harassment among the primary use cases.

The Impact of AI-Driven Manipulation on Society

The societal impact of AI-driven manipulation, including fake news and deepfakes, is profound. These technologies can:

- **Undermine Trust**: When people can no longer trust the information they see, hear, or read, it erodes trust in the media, government, and even personal relationships. Deepfakes, in particular, blur the line between truth and fiction, making it increasingly difficult for individuals to discern what is real and what is not.

- **Polarize Communities**: AI-powered disinformation can target specific groups, inflaming divisions and deepening political and social polarization. This can lead to increased tension, conflict, and a fractured society, where civil discourse becomes impossible.

- **Damage Reputations**: Deepfakes and false information can be used to damage the reputations of individuals, particularly public figures and celebrities. A single fake video or news story can go viral, permanently tarnishing someone's image even after the truth is revealed.

- **Influence Elections and Democracy**: The use of AI-driven manipulation in elections poses a serious threat to democracy. Fake news and deepfakes can be used to mislead voters, spread disinformation about candidates, and disrupt the democratic process. The **2024 International Election Integrity Report** noted that AI-driven manipulation campaigns have been detected in **17%** of elections globally, significantly undermining trust in democratic institutions.

Coping with the Challenges of AI-Driven Deception

To combat the growing threat of AI-driven manipulation, fake news, and deepfakes, a multi-pronged approach is needed—one that involves governments, businesses, technology developers, and individuals working together to ensure that AI is used responsibly and ethically.

- **AI Detection Tools**: One of the most effective ways to combat deepfakes and AI-driven disinformation is through the development of **AI detection technologies**. AI-powered tools can be used to identify and flag manipulated content by analyzing subtle inconsistencies in audio, video, and text. For instance, **Deeptrace** and **Sensity AI** are among the companies developing AI systems capable of detecting deepfakes with **90% accuracy** as of 2024. These tools can help platforms and institutions identify and take down harmful content before it goes viral.

- **Media Literacy**: Educating the public about the dangers of fake news, deepfakes, and AI-driven manipulation is crucial in fostering a more informed society. **Media literacy programs** that teach individuals how to critically evaluate information, verify sources, and recognize AI-generated content can help reduce the spread and impact of disinformation. Schools, community organizations, and governments should invest in media literacy education to empower individuals to navigate the digital landscape safely.

- **Government Regulation**: Governments play a critical role in regulating the use of AI technologies and holding individuals and organizations accountable for their misuse. In 2024, several countries — including the United States and the European Union — introduced legislation requiring platforms to label AI-generated content, remove harmful deep fakes, and enforce stricter penalties for spreading disinformation. The **European AI Act**, for instance, mandates that companies must take down harmful AI-generated media within 24 hours of detection or face significant fines.

  The United Arab Emirates (UAE) has also been proactive in this space. Through its National **Artificial Intelligence Strategy 2031**, the UAE aims to ensure responsible AI development and deployment. The UAE established the **Artificial Intelligence Office** and appointed a **Minister of State for AI** to oversee ethical governance and cross-sector AI integration. In line with these efforts, the UAE has issued **guidelines for responsible AI** use, focusing on transparency, human oversight, data privacy, and algorithmic accountability — especially in sensitive sectors like finance, healthcare, and national security. Additionally, the **UAE Cybersecurity Council** works to combat AI-based cyber threats and misinformation, ensuring that AI innovation aligns with national security and ethical standards.

- **Ethical AI Development**: Technology developers have a responsibility to ensure that the AI tools they create are used ethically. Companies like **Microsoft**, **Google**, and **Facebook** have implemented **AI ethics guidelines** that prioritize transparency, accountability, and fairness in AI development. These guidelines include conducting **bias audits**, ensuring that AI models are trained on diverse datasets, and embedding ethical review processes throughout the development lifecycle.

- **Collaboration Between Platforms and Fact-Checkers**: Social media platforms must collaborate with **independent fact-checking organizations** to identify and remove fake news and deepfakes before they spread. Platforms like **Facebook** and **Twitter** have implemented AI-driven systems to flag potential misinformation, but these systems must continue to evolve to keep pace with the rapidly changing landscape of AI manipulation.

Best Practices for Individuals

Individuals can also take steps to protect themselves from AI-driven manipulation:

1. **Verify Information**: Always cross-check the sources of news articles, videos, and images before sharing them.

Be cautious of sensational or outlandish claims, and use trusted news sources.

2. **Be Skeptical of Viral Content**: If a piece of content goes viral, especially on social media, it's worth questioning its authenticity. Deepfakes and fake news are often designed to spread quickly and emotionally engage audiences.

3. **Use AI Tools**: There are now AI-powered tools available that allow individuals to detect deepfakes or verify the authenticity of content. Using these tools can help you stay ahead of potential AI-driven manipulations.

Final Thoughts: The potential for AI to manipulate minds through misinformation, deepfakes, and persuasive algorithms underscores the need for vigilance and ethical responsibility. As we harness AI's power, it's crucial to implement safeguards and cultivate awareness to counteract these dark sides. By understanding these risks, we can develop strategies to protect individuals and society from the harmful influences of AI, ensuring it serves as a force for positive transformation.

Looking Ahead: As we move forward, the importance of ethics in AI becomes paramount. In the next chapter, we'll look into how businesses can innovate responsibly, ensuring AI developments are aligned with ethical principles and societal well-being. We'll explore how responsible AI practices not only mitigate risks but also enhance trust and foster a culture of integrity within digital transformation initiatives.

14
Ethical AI and Responsible Innovation

"Innovation without ethics is progress without purpose."

As AI becomes increasingly embedded in our daily lives, the question of ethics has moved to the forefront of discussions about its development and use. AI has the power to drive innovation, improve efficiency, and enhance decision-making, but it also poses significant ethical challenges. From issues of **bias** and **privacy** to concerns about **transparency** and **accountability**, the importance of ensuring that AI systems are developed and deployed responsibly cannot be overstated. In this chapter, we'll explore the key ethical considerations in AI, the importance of building **fair** and **transparent** AI systems, and the best practices for organizations to follow to ensure **responsible innovation**.

The Growing Importance of Ethical AI

AI is a transformative technology, but it is also **inherently biased**—not because of the algorithms themselves, but because the data used to train AI models reflects human biases and societal inequalities. Without proper oversight, AI systems can unintentionally reinforce these biases, leading to unfair outcomes that disproportionately affect certain groups of people.

For example, AI systems used in **hiring, loan approvals**, or **criminal justice** can exhibit bias based on race, gender, or socioeconomic status, often reflecting historical patterns of discrimination. A **2023 study by MIT** found that facial recognition algorithms were less accurate at identifying people with darker skin tones, raising concerns about the fairness of AI-powered surveillance and law enforcement technologies.

As AI becomes more widely used in critical areas such as healthcare, education, finance, and criminal justice, the need for

ethical guidelines and **regulatory frameworks** has become urgent. In response, governments, businesses, and academic institutions have begun to develop **AI ethics principles** to ensure that AI is used in a way that promotes fairness, transparency, and accountability.

Ensuring Fairness in AI

One of the primary ethical challenges in AI is ensuring **fairness**—the idea that AI systems should provide equal and unbiased outcomes for all individuals, regardless of race, gender, age, or background. AI fairness involves not only addressing biases in the data but also ensuring that the algorithms themselves are designed to avoid **discriminatory outcomes**.

To achieve fairness in AI, organizations must implement **bias mitigation strategies** throughout the AI development lifecycle. This includes auditing datasets to identify and address potential biases, training AI models on diverse and representative data, and regularly testing AI systems for fairness.

Example of Fairness: Microsoft's AI Fairness Toolkit Microsoft has developed a set of tools and guidelines known as the **AI Fairness Checklist**, which helps developers identify and mitigate bias in AI models. The toolkit includes fairness metrics, testing frameworks, and best practices for training AI systems on diverse datasets. By using these tools, Microsoft ensures that its AI-driven products, such as its **Azure AI platform**, deliver fair and equitable outcomes for all users.

In addition to developing fair AI systems, companies must also ensure that the outcomes generated by AI are **interpretable** and **explainable**. This means that AI systems should be able to provide clear and understandable explanations for their decisions, particularly when those decisions have a significant impact on individuals' lives.

Transparency and Explainability in AI

One of the major concerns surrounding AI is its **opacity**—often referred to as the "black box" problem. Many AI systems, particularly those that rely on deep learning, are so complex that it can be difficult to understand how they arrive at their decisions. This lack of transparency can undermine trust in AI, especially in sensitive areas such as healthcare, finance, and legal systems.

To build trust in AI, organizations must prioritize **transparency** and **explainability**. This involves making AI systems more understandable and accountable, ensuring that stakeholders can see how decisions are made and have the ability to challenge or appeal those decisions if necessary.

Example of Transparency: **Google's Explainable AI** Google has made significant strides in improving the explainability of its AI systems through its **Explainable AI** initiative. The initiative provides developers with tools to create AI models that are transparent and interpretable. For instance, Google's **What-If Tool** allows developers to explore how different inputs affect an AI model's predictions, helping them better understand how the model works and ensuring that it behaves as expected.

Explainability is particularly important in **high-stakes environments** like healthcare, where AI is used to assist with medical diagnoses or treatment recommendations. Patients and doctors need to understand how an AI system arrived at its conclusions in order to make informed decisions. By prioritizing transparency, organizations can build trust in AI and promote ethical decision-making.

Data Privacy and Security in AI

As AI systems increasingly rely on vast amounts of personal data to generate insights and predictions, concerns about **data privacy** have become more pronounced. AI can collect, analyze, and store sensitive information about individuals, including their location, financial history, and health records. If this data is mishandled or misused, it can lead to significant privacy violations and security breaches.

To address these concerns, organizations must ensure that their AI systems comply with **data privacy regulations** such as the **General Data Protection Regulation (GDPR)** and the **California Consumer Privacy Act (CCPA)**. This includes implementing robust data protection measures, providing individuals with control over their personal data, and ensuring that AI systems only collect and use data for legitimate purposes.

Example of Data Privacy: Apple's Commitment to Privacy
Apple has made privacy a core principle of its AI development, ensuring that its AI-powered products, such as **Siri** and **Face ID**, are designed with privacy in mind. Apple's **differential privacy** approach allows the company to collect data while ensuring that individual user identities are protected. By minimizing data collection and implementing strong encryption, Apple has built AI systems that prioritize user privacy while still delivering powerful capabilities.

In addition to protecting personal data, organizations must also take steps to secure their AI systems against **cyberattacks**. As AI becomes more integrated into critical infrastructure, the risk of AI-driven cyberattacks increases. Ensuring that AI systems are secure and resilient to threats is essential for maintaining trust in AI technologies.

Accountability and Governance in AI

For AI to be used ethically, there must be **clear accountability** for its outcomes. This means that organizations must establish governance frameworks that hold AI developers, operators, and users accountable for the actions and decisions made by AI systems. Governance frameworks should include guidelines for auditing AI systems, monitoring their performance, and ensuring that they comply with ethical standards.

To promote accountability, companies should implement **AI ethics committees** or **AI governance boards** that oversee the development and deployment of AI technologies. These committees should include diverse stakeholders, such as ethicists, legal experts, and representatives from marginalized communities, to ensure that a wide range of perspectives is considered when making decisions about AI ethics.

Example of AI Governance: Facebook's Oversight Board
In response to growing concerns about the ethical use of AI and algorithms on its platform, Facebook established an independent **Oversight Board** to review decisions related to content moderation and AI-driven systems. The board has the authority to review and overturn decisions made by Facebook's algorithms,

ensuring that the company's AI systems operate in a transparent, fair, and accountable manner.

Building a Culture of Responsible Innovation

Organizations must foster a culture of **responsible innovation**—one that emphasizes the importance of ethics, fairness, and transparency in AI development. This requires companies to go beyond simply complying with regulations and actively seek to mitigate the potential harms of AI. By embedding ethical considerations into the AI development process, businesses can ensure that their AI solutions are not only innovative but also socially responsible.

Key steps for building a culture of responsible innovation include:

1. **Incorporating Ethics into AI Design**: Ethical considerations should be integrated into every stage of AI development, from data collection and algorithm design to deployment and monitoring. This includes assessing the potential impact of AI systems on different populations and ensuring that the benefits of AI are shared equitably.

2. **Engaging Diverse Stakeholders**: To ensure that AI systems are fair and inclusive, organizations must engage with a diverse range of stakeholders, including underrepresented groups and communities that may be disproportionately affected by AI technologies. This helps to identify potential biases and unintended consequences early in the development process.

3. **Continuous Monitoring and Improvement**: AI systems should be continuously monitored and audited to ensure that they are performing as expected and that any ethical concerns are addressed in a timely manner. This includes regularly updating AI models to reflect new data and societal changes.

Final Thoughts: As AI continues to shape the future, ensuring that it is developed and used ethically will be one of the most important challenges for businesses, governments, and society as a whole. By prioritizing fairness, transparency, privacy, and accountability, we can build a future where AI serves as a force for good—driving innovation while protecting human rights and promoting social justice.

Looking Ahead: As organizations deepen their digital transformation journeys, the need for robust cybersecurity becomes critical. In the next chapter, we'll explore how AI is reshaping cybersecurity strategies, offering innovative solutions to protect digital assets and maintain trust in an increasingly interconnected world. From threat detection to incident response, AI's role in cybersecurity is pivotal to safeguarding the future of digital transformation.

15
Cybersecurity in Digital Transformation

"In the digital age, security is not a feature—it's the foundation."

As organizations worldwide embark on digital transformation, cybersecurity has become a top priority. In this ever-evolving landscape, artificial intelligence (AI) plays a dual role: it is both a powerful tool for defending against cyber threats and a potential enabler of more sophisticated attacks. This chapter explores AI's complex role in cybersecurity within the broader context of digital transformation, examining the opportunities and risks it brings.

AI as a Tool for Cyber Defense

The complexity and frequency of cyberattacks have surged in recent years, often overwhelming traditional security systems. As businesses digitize their operations, their attack surfaces expand, leaving them vulnerable to increasingly sophisticated threats. AI-driven cybersecurity solutions offer a way to tackle these challenges, revolutionizing how organizations protect their systems, data, and networks.

AI can process vast amounts of data at speeds and with precision that exceed human capabilities. This makes it exceptionally effective in identifying and responding to threats. For example, AI-powered systems leverage machine learning (ML) algorithms to detect unusual patterns and behaviors that may signal an intrusion. According to Gartner's 2024 report, 60% of enterprises that implemented AI-driven cybersecurity solutions reported a 30% reduction in successful cyberattacks.

These AI systems can analyze diverse data sources in real-time—such as logs, network traffic, and threat intelligence—to detect and neutralize threats. IBM's Watson for Cyber Security, for instance, can sift through billions of data points to identify potential threats with a high degree of accuracy. By analyzing historical attack data, these systems also continuously learn and adapt, enhancing their ability to detect even subtle anomalies that could indicate an impending attack.

AI in Threat Detection and Incident Response

One of AI's most significant contributions to cybersecurity is in the area of threat detection. Traditional security systems often rely on signature-based detection, which requires a database of known malware signatures to identify threats. While effective against known threats, this approach leaves organizations vulnerable to zero-day attacks—exploits that target previously unknown vulnerabilities.

AI, however, uses behavioral analysis and anomaly detection to identify unusual activities that may signal a threat, even if it has never been seen before. For instance, AI can detect a spike in login attempts from a suspicious location or an unusual increase in data transfer activity. By flagging these behaviors for further investigation, AI helps organizations uncover threats before they can escalate into full-blown attacks.

AI also transforms incident response by enabling real-time action. Automated AI-driven systems can respond to threats as they unfold, reducing the time it takes to contain and mitigate potential damage. Endpoint detection and response (EDR) solutions, for example, can isolate infected devices, prevent malware from spreading, and initiate automated remediation actions. According to Forrester's 2023 Cybersecurity Trends Report, organizations that leverage AI for incident response report a 40% reduction in the time required to contain security incidents.

The Dark Side of AI in Cybersecurity

While AI enhances defense, it also presents new challenges as cybercriminals harness AI for their own purposes. These AI-driven cyberattacks are becoming more common and sophisticated, complicating the digital landscape. Cybercriminals are now able to deploy AI to automate attacks on a scale that was previously unimaginable.

One of the most concerning developments is the use of AI to scan networks for vulnerabilities at an accelerated rate. Attackers can leverage AI algorithms to identify weaknesses in a target's infrastructure, prioritize these vulnerabilities, and even automate the execution of attacks. AI-powered bots can also conduct phishing campaigns by generating convincing and highly personalized messages, which are more difficult to detect than traditional phishing attempts. The ability to personalize these attacks makes them more effective, as recipients are more likely to trust messages that appear relevant to them.

AI has also enabled the creation of polymorphic malware, which constantly changes its code to evade traditional signature-based detection systems. Such malware can adapt its behavior based on its environment, making it extremely difficult for cybersecurity systems to identify and mitigate. Additionally, AI-generated deepfakes are being used in cybercrime, especially in social engineering attacks. For example, a 2023 case involved a deepfake of a CEO's voice used to convince an employee to authorize a $10 million transfer to a fraudulent account, underscoring the risks of AI in the hands of bad actors.

Strengthening Cybersecurity in Digital Transformation

Given the dual role of AI, organizations must adopt a multi-faceted approach to cybersecurity, particularly as they undergo digital transformation. Key strategies include:

1. **Adopting AI-Driven Security Solutions:** AI-powered tools enhance defense mechanisms by providing continuous monitoring, detecting threats in real-time, and automating responses. AI-driven intrusion prevention systems (IPS), for instance, can automatically block suspicious activities, reducing the likelihood of successful attacks.

2. **Human-AI Collaboration:** While AI can enhance cybersecurity, it should complement rather than replace human expertise. A collaborative approach where AI tools work alongside human security teams is most effective. According to McKinsey's 2024 Cybersecurity Report, organizations that blend AI with human intelligence achieve 30% greater effectiveness in preventing breaches. By handling routine tasks, AI frees up security analysts to focus on complex, strategic issues that require human insight.

3. **Regular Audits and Threat Assessments:** With AI-driven attacks on the rise, organizations should conduct regular security audits and threat assessments. AI can help by scanning networks for weaknesses, while human oversight ensures a thorough review. Red team-blue team exercises—simulated attacks—can test defenses against advanced threats, providing valuable insights for improving security posture.

4. **Protecting AI Systems from Adversarial Attacks:** As organizations increasingly rely on AI for cybersecurity, protecting these AI systems from adversarial attacks becomes essential. Adversarial attacks can feed misleading data into AI models, causing them to make incorrect decisions. Organizations must implement encryption, data validation, and frequent updates to AI algorithms to secure their AI infrastructure.

5. **Enhancing Cyber Threat Intelligence:** AI can analyze global threat data to identify emerging trends and predict potential attack vectors. By leveraging AI-driven threat intelligence platforms, organizations can anticipate attacks and proactively strengthen defenses. According to FireEye's 2024 data, organizations using AI for threat intelligence experience a 25% reduction in the time to detect and respond to threats, staying a step ahead of cybercriminals.

The Future of Cybersecurity in Digital Transformation

As AI technology continues to advance, we can expect to see more autonomous systems capable of preemptively predicting and preventing cyberattacks. These systems will use advanced machine learning algorithms to anticipate hacker behaviors and fortify defenses ahead of time, providing a powerful layer of protection as organizations adapt to digital transformation.

However, the rise of AI-powered cyber threats means organizations must remain vigilant. The future of cybersecurity will require continuous investment in research and development, the adoption of cutting-edge technologies, and a strong culture of cybersecurity awareness. By integrating these elements into their digital transformation strategies, businesses can better safeguard their digital assets.

Final Thoughts: As digital transformation advances, cybersecurity emerges as a cornerstone for sustainable growth and resilience. AI enhances security measures, enabling faster detection and response to evolving threats. Yet, as AI strengthens defenses, it also introduces new vulnerabilities. Organizations must balance innovation with vigilance, leveraging AI to not only protect their assets but also to build a foundation of trust in the digital age. This ongoing commitment to cybersecurity will be vital for any successful digital transformation journey.

Looking Ahead: With the groundwork laid in previous chapters, we now turn to the best practices that can guide organizations toward successful digital transformation. Chapter 16 we'll explore best practices and actionable strategies that businesses can follow to ensure the success of their digital transformation initiatives. We'll also examine real-world examples of both successful and failed transformations, offering key takeaways for organizations looking to thrive in the digital age.

16

Best Practices for a Successful Digital Transformation

"Success in transformation lies not in tools but in principles and people."

In today's fast-paced business landscape, digital transformation is no longer an option—it's a necessity. Organizations are turning to **artificial intelligence (AI)** and other advanced technologies to drive innovation, improve efficiency, and stay competitive. However, embarking on a digital transformation journey can be complex and fraught with challenges. In this chapter, we'll explore **best practices** and actionable strategies that businesses can follow to ensure the success of their digital transformation initiatives. We'll also examine real-world examples of both successful and failed transformations, offering key takeaways for organizations looking to thrive in the digital age.

1. Start with a Clear Vision and Strategy

The foundation of a successful digital transformation is a **clear vision** and **well-defined strategy**. Before diving into AI or other digital technologies, organizations must understand why they are pursuing transformation and what they hope to achieve. Without a clear purpose, digital transformation initiatives can lose focus and fail to deliver the desired outcomes.

A successful digital transformation strategy should be **aligned with the company's broader business goals** and **customer-centric**. For example, is the goal to improve operational efficiency, enhance customer experiences, or develop new products and services? Understanding the "why" behind digital transformation allows businesses to set measurable objectives and guide decision-making throughout the process.

Example of Success: **Nike's Digital Transformation** Nike successfully transformed itself from a traditional retail brand to a technology-driven company by focusing on a clear vision:

delivering personalized and seamless customer experiences. The company invested in AI-powered data analytics, which helped it predict consumer trends, manage inventory, and optimize supply chains. Nike's commitment to its digital strategy resulted in a **35% increase in direct-to-consumer sales** and a stronger connection with customers.

2. Prioritize Customer Experience

Digital transformation is not just about adopting new technologies—it's about **enhancing customer experiences**. AI and digital tools should be implemented with the goal of improving how businesses interact with and serve their customers. A **customer-first approach** ensures that digital transformation initiatives are designed to meet customer needs and expectations, leading to higher satisfaction and loyalty.

By leveraging AI, businesses can deliver **personalized experiences**, such as targeted marketing, tailored product recommendations, and seamless customer support. For example, AI-powered chatbots can provide real-time assistance to customers, improving response times and reducing support costs.

Example of Failure: **JCPenney's Digital Transformation Misstep** JCPenney, a once-prominent department store chain, struggled with its digital transformation efforts due to a lack of focus on customer experience. The company invested in technology but failed to align its digital initiatives with customer preferences. JCPenney's attempts to overhaul its pricing strategy and online presence led to confusion among customers, ultimately resulting in a **decline in sales** and store closures.

3. Foster an AI-Ready Culture

As we explored in previous chapters, fostering an **AI-ready culture** is crucial for digital transformation success. This means cultivating a **digital-first mindset** across the organization and ensuring that employees are prepared to work alongside AI technologies. Resistance to change is one of the biggest barriers to digital transformation, so companies must prioritize **employee training** and **upskilling** to bridge the digital skills gap.

Leaders must also champion AI adoption and create a culture where **experimentation** and **innovation** are encouraged. Cross-functional collaboration between AI specialists, business leaders, and other departments is essential for driving successful digital initiatives. According to a **2024 McKinsey survey**, organizations that invest in developing a culture of digital innovation are **2.7 times more likely** to achieve successful digital transformation outcomes.

Example of Success: **Walmart's Digital Innovation Culture** Walmart embraced a digital-first culture by investing in AI-powered supply chain automation and data analytics to optimize inventory management and improve customer experiences. The company also upskilled its workforce, training employees to use AI tools to improve operational efficiency. As a result, Walmart significantly reduced inventory shortages and achieved **24% growth in e-commerce sales**.

4. Focus on Agile Implementation

Digital transformation is an ongoing journey, not a one-time event. To ensure long-term success, organizations should adopt an **agile implementation** approach. This involves rolling out digital initiatives in **phases**, testing and refining solutions along the way, and scaling successful projects. Agile implementation allows businesses to adapt to changing market conditions and customer needs while minimizing risks associated with large-scale technology rollouts.

Instead of implementing AI across the entire organization all at once, companies can start with **pilot projects** that test AI solutions in specific departments or processes. Once these pilots demonstrate value, the company can scale the solutions to other parts of the business.

Example of Success: **Rolls-Royce's AI-Powered Maintenance System** Rolls-Royce took an agile approach to digital transformation by piloting its **AI-powered predictive maintenance** system for its aircraft engines. The system uses AI to monitor engine performance and predict maintenance needs before failures occur. After a successful pilot, Rolls-Royce scaled the solution across its fleet, reducing maintenance costs and improving engine reliability. The company's agile approach ensured that the AI solution was continuously optimized and adapted to different aircraft models.

5. Leverage Data for Decision Making

Data is the fuel that powers digital transformation. AI and machine learning algorithms rely on vast amounts of data to generate insights and drive decision-making. Therefore, organizations must prioritize **data collection**, **management**, and **analysis** to unlock the full potential of AI technologies. This requires building a robust **data infrastructure** and ensuring that data is collected, stored, and processed in a way that complies with privacy regulations like the **General Data Protection Regulation (GDPR)**.

In addition to leveraging historical data, businesses should adopt **real-time data analytics** to make faster, more informed decisions. By analyzing data in real time, companies can respond to market changes, customer behavior, and operational challenges more effectively.

Example of Failure: **Sears' Missed Data Opportunity** Sears, once a retail giant, missed the opportunity to leverage data analytics in its digital transformation efforts. Despite having access to vast amounts of customer data, the company failed to invest in data-driven technologies that could have provided insights into changing consumer preferences. As competitors like Amazon and Walmart embraced AI and data analytics, Sears struggled to keep up, leading to a **significant decline in sales** and eventual bankruptcy.

6. Ensure Cybersecurity and Data Privacy

As companies adopt AI and other digital technologies, **cybersecurity** and **data privacy** must remain a top priority. Digital transformation introduces new vulnerabilities, and organizations must take steps to protect their systems, data, and customers from cyber threats. This includes implementing **AI-driven cybersecurity solutions**, conducting regular **security audits**, and ensuring compliance with data protection regulations.

Businesses must also be transparent about how they collect and use customer data. Customers are becoming increasingly aware of privacy issues, and companies that fail to protect customer data can face severe reputational and financial consequences.

Example of Success: Salesforce's Commitment to Cybersecurity Salesforce has successfully integrated AI into its platform while maintaining a strong focus on cybersecurity and data privacy. The company uses AI-driven security solutions to monitor and protect customer data and ensures that its products comply with global data protection regulations. Salesforce's proactive approach to cybersecurity has helped it build trust with customers and maintain its position as a leading CRM platform.

7. Learn from Failures and Iterate

Not every digital transformation initiative will be a success, and that's okay. What matters is how organizations learn from their failures and iterate to improve future efforts. **Failing fast** and learning from mistakes is a key principle of digital transformation, allowing businesses to refine their strategies and avoid repeating the same errors.

Companies should conduct **post-mortem analyses** of failed projects to identify what went wrong and what can be improved. This culture of continuous improvement fosters resilience and positions organizations to succeed in their long-term digital transformation journeys.

Example of Failure: GE's Overly Ambitious Digital Transformation General Electric (GE) embarked on an ambitious digital transformation journey with the launch of its **Predix** platform, which aimed to connect industrial equipment to the internet and provide data analytics for GE's clients. However, GE's efforts were plagued by overly ambitious goals, a lack of clear direction, and insufficient investment in AI infrastructure. Predix failed to gain traction, resulting in significant financial losses for GE. The company later scaled back its digital efforts, learning from its missteps and refocusing its strategy on more manageable goals.

Final Thoughts: Successful digital transformation requires a combination of **vision**, **culture**, and **execution**. By following these best practices—starting with a clear strategy, prioritizing customer experience, fostering an AI-ready culture, and leveraging data—organizations can navigate the complexities of digital transformation and achieve meaningful results. As AI and other technologies continue to evolve, businesses that remain agile, data-driven, and customer-focused will be well-positioned to thrive in the digital age.

Looking Ahead: As we explore the evolving relationship between AI and the workplace, Chapter 17 will focus on how AI is reshaping the future of work. We'll examine how AI-driven automation, augmented intelligence, and new skill requirements are transforming jobs across industries. This chapter will provide insights into what these changes mean for both employees and organizations, helping you understand how to prepare for a workforce where human and artificial intelligence coexist harmoniously, driving productivity and innovation to new heights.

17
AI and the Future of Work

"AI won't replace jobs—it will redefine how we create value."

As artificial intelligence (AI) continues to advance, it is transforming the job market and reshaping the way we work. While some fear that AI will lead to widespread job displacement, the reality is more complex. AI is not only automating tasks but also creating new opportunities for innovation, upskilling, and job creation. In this chapter, we'll explore how AI is **redefining roles**, the impact it has on different industries, and the steps businesses and workers can take to adapt to the **future of work**.

The Dual Impact of AI on the Workforce

AI has the potential to both disrupt and enhance the workforce. On one hand, automation is replacing certain repetitive and manual tasks, which can lead to job displacement in industries such as manufacturing, retail, and customer service. On the other hand, AI is also creating new opportunities by generating demand for **AI-driven roles** and reshaping existing jobs.

According to a **2024 World Economic Forum (WEF) report**, AI is expected to displace **85 million jobs** by 2025, but it will also create **97 million new roles** in fields such as data science, AI engineering, and machine learning. This shift represents a significant transformation in the job market, where routine tasks are increasingly automated while **high-skill, creative, and strategic roles** continue to grow in importance.

The key challenge for businesses and workers alike is to adapt to this new reality. As AI automates repetitive tasks, workers must embrace opportunities to **upskill**, reskill, and develop the critical thinking and problem-solving skills needed to thrive in an AI-powered economy.

Redefining Roles in the Age of AI

AI is not just automating jobs—it is also **augmenting** them. In many industries, AI is being used to assist workers, enabling them to perform their roles more efficiently and focus on higher-value tasks. This shift is particularly evident in professions that require a combination of **technical expertise** and **human judgment**.

For example, in **healthcare**, AI is being used to assist doctors and medical professionals in diagnosing diseases and analyzing medical data. AI-driven tools can analyze medical images and patient records, allowing doctors to make more accurate diagnoses and provide personalized treatment plans. However, while AI can assist with data analysis, it cannot replace the **empathy** and **critical thinking** that doctors provide when interacting with patients.

In **finance**, AI-powered algorithms are helping analysts sift through massive amounts of financial data to identify trends, optimize portfolios, and detect fraudulent transactions. By automating these tasks, AI frees financial professionals to focus on strategy, client relationships, and risk management.

Even in **creative industries**, AI is enhancing roles rather than replacing them. AI tools can assist designers, writers, and artists by generating ideas, suggesting improvements, or automating certain aspects of production. For example, AI-driven design platforms like **Adobe Sensei** help graphic designers streamline their workflows and experiment with new design concepts. Similarly, AI tools for writers can generate content outlines, suggest phrasing, and improve the efficiency of the writing process.

Industries Most Impacted by AI

AI's impact on the workforce varies by industry, with certain sectors experiencing more profound changes than others. Here are some of the industries most affected by AI:

1. **Manufacturing**: AI-driven robotics and automation have transformed the manufacturing industry by streamlining production processes, reducing errors, and improving efficiency. Smart factories, powered by AI, are capable of running 24/7 with minimal human intervention. However, this shift has led to job displacement for workers in manual roles, while creating new opportunities for those skilled in **robotics maintenance**, **AI programming**, and **data analysis**.

2. **Retail**: In the retail sector, AI is being used to optimize supply chains, manage inventory, and personalize customer experiences. AI-powered chatbots and virtual shopping assistants provide real-time customer support, while machine learning algorithms predict demand and optimize pricing. As AI automates many aspects of retail operations, roles in **customer service**, **sales**, and **logistics** are evolving to focus on **relationship-building** and **customer experience**.

3. **Healthcare**: AI's ability to analyze medical data and predict patient outcomes is revolutionizing healthcare. AI-powered diagnostic tools assist doctors in identifying diseases earlier and with greater accuracy, while predictive analytics tools help hospitals manage resources more

efficiently. As AI takes on more administrative and data-driven tasks, healthcare professionals can focus on patient care and complex medical decision-making.

4. **Finance**: The financial services industry is increasingly relying on AI to improve risk management, automate trading, and detect fraud. AI-powered robo-advisors provide personalized investment advice, while algorithms analyze vast amounts of financial data to generate insights. However, AI's rise in finance has also raised concerns about **job displacement** for traditional financial analysts and advisors, requiring these professionals to adapt by developing more specialized skills.

The Role of Upskilling and Reskilling

As AI reshapes the workforce, the importance of **upskilling** and **reskilling** cannot be overstated. To remain competitive in the job market, workers must acquire new skills that complement AI technologies and position them for the **jobs of the future**. This includes developing skills in **data analysis**, **AI programming**, **cybersecurity**, and **digital literacy**.

Businesses also have a responsibility to support their employees through this transition. Companies should invest in **training programs** and provide opportunities for workers to learn new skills. According to a **2023 McKinsey study**, companies that prioritize upskilling their workforce are **2.5 times more likely** to successfully integrate AI into their operations. Furthermore, workers who actively pursue upskilling are more likely to secure higher-paying, more fulfilling roles in the evolving job market.

Example of Success: **Amazon's Upskilling 2025 Initiative**
Amazon recognized the need to prepare its workforce for the future of work by launching the **Upskilling 2025** initiative, which aims to invest over $700 million to provide training for more than 100,000 employees. This initiative offers training programs in fields such as data science, machine learning, and robotics, enabling employees to transition to higher-skill roles within the company. By investing in upskilling, Amazon is ensuring that its workforce is prepared for the AI-driven future.

Innovation and Job Creation in the AI Era

While AI is automating certain tasks, it is also driving **innovation** and creating new jobs in fields that didn't exist a decade ago. For example, roles in **AI ethics**, **machine learning engineering**, and **data science** are in high demand as organizations seek to develop, deploy, and manage AI systems responsibly.

AI is also fueling the rise of **gig economy** platforms and **remote work**, providing new opportunities for individuals to offer specialized services in a flexible work environment. Freelancers skilled in AI programming, content creation, digital marketing, and graphic design are leveraging online platforms to connect with clients around the world, creating new business models and income streams.

In addition to creating new job roles, AI is driving **entrepreneurial opportunities**. Startups in AI-driven industries such as autonomous vehicles, biotechnology, and fintech are rapidly emerging, offering new avenues for innovation and job creation. The **AI startup ecosystem** has seen explosive growth, with **global**

AI startups raising over $50 billion in venture capital funding in 2023, according to **CB Insights**.

Preparing for the Future of Work

To thrive in the AI-driven workforce, both businesses and individuals must embrace **lifelong learning** and **adaptability**. As AI continues to evolve, the skills needed to succeed in the job market will continue to change. This means that workers must be willing to continuously learn and adapt to new technologies, while businesses must foster a culture of **innovation**, **creativity**, and **collaboration**.

Governments also play a crucial role in preparing the workforce for the future of work. Policymakers must invest in education and training programs that equip workers with the skills needed for the AI era. This includes expanding access to **STEM education**, providing financial support for vocational training, and encouraging public-private partnerships to drive innovation in workforce development.

Final Thoughts: AI is transforming the workforce in ways that are both exciting and challenging. While automation may displace some jobs, AI is also creating new opportunities for innovation, upskilling, and job creation. As AI continues to reshape industries, the future of work will depend on our ability to **adapt** and **embrace change**. By investing in education, upskilling, and responsible innovation, businesses and individuals can harness the potential of AI to create a more **dynamic**, **inclusive**, and **resilient** workforce.

Looking Ahead: In the next chapter, we will explore how AI is revolutionizing the workplace, unlocking its potential to transform mental well-being and create healthier environments. By integrating human empathy with AI's precision, organizations can achieve a harmonious balance that elevates both productivity and employee well-being. This chapter marks the beginning of a journey toward AI-driven workplaces that empower and inspire.

18
AI and Mental Well-being: Building Healthier Workplaces

"When minds and machines harmonize, the workplace fosters productivity and well-being."

As AI becomes a co-creator in the workplace symphony, its role in mental well-being and creating harmonious environments is instrumental. This chapter dives deep into the transformative potential of AI in redefining how we work, connect, and thrive.

The Evolving Workplace in the AI Era

The workplace is no longer just a physical space where tasks are completed; it has transformed into a dynamic ecosystem where technology and human creativity intersect. AI plays a dual role in this transformation—both as a disruptor and as an enabler of well-being.

While AI systems automate tasks, analyze data, and enhance productivity, they also introduce stressors such as the fear of obsolescence and the pressure to continuously adapt. Yet, this very technology offers solutions to these challenges. By using AI to understand and support mental well-being, organizations can create an environment where employees feel valued, supported, and empowered.

This chapter explores how AI and human intelligence can harmonize to address mental health challenges, fostering workplaces that inspire innovation and nurture the human spirit.

1. Understanding Mental Well-being in the AI Era

Mental well-being encompasses more than just the absence of mental illness; it is about thriving in one's environment, finding fulfillment in work, and maintaining a balance between professional and personal life.

Challenges Introduced by AI-Driven Workplaces:

A. Fear of Job Displacement: The automation of repetitive tasks has sparked widespread concerns about job security, particularly in industries where AI adoption is rapid.

- **Example:** Manufacturing and logistics sectors have seen significant disruptions due to AI-powered robotics and predictive systems.

B. Pressure to Upskill Continuously:

- Employees are now expected to adapt to new tools and AI systems regularly. This constant demand for learning can lead to anxiety and a feeling of inadequacy.

C. Digital Overload:

- Always-on digital communication tools, many enhanced by AI, blur the boundaries between work and personal life, contributing to burnout.

Understanding these challenges is the first step in leveraging AI to address them effectively.

2. AI as a Solution for Mental Health

AI offers a range of tools and applications designed to support mental well-being, making it a critical ally in addressing workplace challenges.

A. Personalized Mental Health Tools:

AI applications such as *Woebot* and *Wysa* demonstrate how technology can simulate empathetic conversations, guide users through mindfulness exercises, and provide instant support.

- **Unique Strengths:**

  - Accessibility: Available 24/7, offering immediate relief during stressful moments.

  - Anonymity: Reduces the stigma often associated with seeking mental health support.

  - Scalability: Organizations can implement these tools at scale to support entire workforces.

B. Early Detection of Mental Health Issues:

AI systems excel in identifying patterns that may indicate stress or burnout.

- **How it Works:**

  - Analyzing communication trends in emails or chats to detect frustration or disengagement.

  - Monitoring productivity data to identify dips that could signal burnout.

- **Example:**

  - A tech company used an AI tool to monitor employee engagement, identifying teams under high stress and providing tailored well-being interventions, resulting in a 20% increase in morale.

C. AI-Powered Coaching and Counseling:

AI-enhanced Employee Assistance Programs (EAPs) provide:

- Real-time advice on workload management.

- Stress management techniques tailored to individual needs.

- Virtual counseling sessions for remote employees.

These tools act as proactive partners in mental health management, addressing issues before they escalate.

3. AI's Role in Creating Healthier Work Environments

AI is reshaping workplaces to prioritize not just productivity but also the well-being of employees.

A. Smart Workplaces:

AI transforms the physical workplace into a responsive and adaptive environment.

- **Examples:**

  - AI-powered desks that adjust ergonomically to reduce physical strain.

  - Smart lighting systems that mimic natural light cycles to enhance mood and focus.

  - Health-monitoring wearables that provide real-time feedback on stress and fatigue levels.

B. Enhancing Team Collaboration:

AI collaboration tools streamline communication and reduce workplace friction.

- Features like automated meeting summaries, real-time language translation, and sentiment analysis during discussions ensure teams remain aligned and productive.

C. Diversity and Inclusion:

AI tools promote equity by analyzing hiring practices, identifying biases, and ensuring fair treatment across all levels of the organization.

- **Case Study:**

  - A global corporation used AI to analyze hiring data, discovering unconscious bias in job descriptions. The corrections led to a 25% increase in diverse hires.

4. AI and Work-Life Balance

AI has the potential to restore work-life harmony by automating routine tasks and providing tools for better time management.

- **Automated Assistants:**

  - Virtual assistants, like Google Assistant and Microsoft Viva, help employees organize their schedules, reminding them to take breaks and prioritize tasks.

- **Task Prioritization Systems:**

  - AI-driven platforms analyze workloads, highlight urgent tasks, and identify areas where delegation is possible.

- **Employee Empowerment:**

  - By handling repetitive tasks, AI allows employees to focus on creativity and strategic thinking, fostering a sense of fulfillment and reducing stress.

5. Ethical Considerations

The integration of AI in workplace well-being requires careful ethical considerations to ensure trust and transparency.

- **Privacy:**
  - Employee data collected by AI tools must be anonymized and securely stored.

- **Transparency:**
  - Organizations should clearly communicate how AI tools are used and their benefits to employees.

- **Bias Management:**
  - Ensuring that AI models used for hiring or mental health analysis are free from biases that could inadvertently harm employees.

6. Future Trends in AI for Mental Well-being

AI's role in mental health and workplace well-being is only beginning to unfold. Emerging trends include:

- **Immersive Therapy with AI-Driven VR:**
  - Virtual reality environments powered by AI can provide immersive stress relief and therapeutic experiences.

- **Predictive AI Models:**
  - AI systems that predict mental health issues based on data patterns and provide early interventions.

- **AI-Neuroadaptive Technologies:**
  - Integrating AI with neuroscience to create systems that adapt in real time to cognitive and emotional states, enhancing workplace engagement and reducing stress.

Final Thoughts: In the symphony of digital transformation, AI plays a crucial role in harmonizing productivity with mental well-being. It empowers organizations to create environments where employees feel supported, valued, and motivated. By embracing this partnership between AI and human intelligence, businesses can ensure that their digital transformation journey is not only efficient but also human-centric.

In the end, the true success of AI-driven workplaces lies in their ability to fuse technology with empathy, creating a symphony where innovation and well-being thrive together.

Looking Ahead: Chapter 19 will bring theory to life by showcasing real-world examples of AI-driven digital transformation across various industries. These case studies highlight how organizations have successfully integrated AI to achieve remarkable outcomes, from enhanced customer experiences to operational efficiencies and sustainability gains. As you explore these stories, you'll gain a deeper appreciation for the tangible impact of AI and uncover valuable lessons that can inspire and guide your own digital transformation journey.

19
Case Studies: AI-Driven Digital Success Stories

"Real transformation isn't theory—it's the stories we create through action."

AI has become the driving force behind digital transformation for many organizations, enabling them to optimize operations, improve customer experiences, and promote sustainability. In this chapter, we will explore **real-world case studies** from leading companies and sectors that have successfully integrated AI to achieve **digital transformation** and **sustainable growth**. These stories highlight the power of AI to create meaningful change across industries, from healthcare and retail to manufacturing and energy.

Case Study 1: Siemens – Transforming Manufacturing with AI and Automation

Industry: Manufacturing

Key Outcome: Increased productivity and reduced energy consumption

Siemens, a global leader in industrial manufacturing, has fully embraced AI and **automation** to transform its production processes. The company's **Amberg Electronics Plant** in Germany is a showcase for the **smart factory** of the future, where **AI-powered systems** manage everything from production planning to quality control.

At the heart of Siemens' success is its use of **predictive maintenance** and **machine learning algorithms**. These AI systems analyze data from thousands of sensors across the factory floor to predict equipment failures before they occur, reducing downtime and minimizing disruptions to the production process. This has resulted in a **99.98% production quality rate**, making the plant one of the most efficient in the world.

Moreover, Siemens has optimized its energy consumption using AI-powered **energy management systems**. These systems track and analyze energy use in real time, identifying areas where energy savings can be made without compromising production quality. By implementing these AI-driven optimizations, Siemens has reduced its **energy consumption by 20%** and significantly lowered its carbon footprint.

Case Study 2: IBM – AI-Driven Healthcare Solutions with Watson Health

Industry: Healthcare

Key Outcome: Enhanced medical diagnoses and improved patient outcomes

IBM's **Watson Health** platform is a prime example of how AI can revolutionize the **healthcare industry**. Watson Health uses AI to analyze massive datasets from medical records, clinical trials, and research studies to help doctors make more informed decisions about patient care. The platform's ability to process unstructured data, such as medical images and research papers, allows it to provide insights that would be difficult or impossible for humans to uncover.

One of Watson Health's most successful applications is in **oncology**. Watson for Oncology analyzes data on millions of cancer cases and treatment outcomes to recommend personalized treatment plans for patients. By identifying the most effective therapies based on each patient's unique genetic makeup and medical history, Watson has improved cancer treatment outcomes and reduced the time doctors spend on research.

In addition to its success in oncology, Watson Health has been used to improve **predictive analytics** in hospitals. AI-powered systems can predict which patients are at risk of developing complications or require intensive care, allowing hospitals to allocate resources more efficiently and improve patient outcomes. As a result, hospitals using Watson Health have seen a **30% reduction in hospital readmission rates** and a significant improvement in overall patient care.

Case Study 3: Amazon – AI-Driven Supply Chain Optimization

Industry: Retail and E-Commerce

Key Outcome: Improved delivery speed and reduced operational costs

Amazon is widely recognized for its innovation in **supply chain management**, and AI plays a critical role in maintaining its position as a global e-commerce leader. The company's use of **machine learning algorithms** and **predictive analytics** has transformed its supply chain, enabling it to forecast demand more accurately, optimize inventory levels, and streamline its distribution network.

Amazon's AI systems continuously analyze purchasing patterns, seasonal trends, and even weather conditions to predict which products will be in demand at specific times and locations. This allows the company to stock the right products in the right warehouses, ensuring that customers receive their orders quickly and efficiently. By optimizing its logistics network using AI, Amazon has reduced delivery times while minimizing transportation costs and fuel consumption.

In addition to its use of AI in logistics, Amazon has implemented **automated robots** in its fulfillment centers to streamline order processing. These robots work alongside human workers to pick, pack, and ship products, speeding up the entire process and reducing the risk of errors. The combination of AI and robotics has enabled Amazon to meet the increasing demand for fast delivery while maintaining high levels of accuracy and efficiency.

Case Study 4: Ørsted – AI-Enhanced Renewable Energy

Industry: Renewable Energy

Key Outcome: Improved wind farm efficiency and increased renewable energy output

Ørsted, a global leader in **renewable energy**, has harnessed the power of AI to improve the efficiency of its **wind farms** and increase its renewable energy output. The company uses AI algorithms to analyze data from wind turbines, weather patterns, and energy markets to optimize the performance of its wind farms.

AI enables Ørsted to predict wind speeds and energy production with greater accuracy, allowing the company to balance supply and demand more effectively. By using **predictive maintenance** powered by AI, Ørsted can detect potential equipment failures before they happen, reducing downtime and maintenance costs. This proactive approach has improved the efficiency of Ørsted's wind turbines by **15%**, ensuring that the company generates more clean energy from its existing infrastructure.

Additionally, Ørsted uses AI to manage its energy trading operations. AI algorithms analyze market conditions in real time and make decisions about when to sell excess energy generated by wind farms. This has allowed Ørsted to maximize its revenue while supporting the integration of renewable energy into the grid.

Case Study 5: Coca-Cola – AI-Driven Consumer Insights and Sustainability

Industry: Food and Beverage

Key Outcome: Improved consumer engagement and reduced environmental impac

Coca-Cola has leveraged AI to both enhance its **customer engagement** and drive **sustainability initiatives**. The company uses **AI-powered analytics** to analyze data from customer interactions, social media, and sales trends to gain deep insights into consumer preferences. These insights allow Coca-Cola to develop personalized marketing campaigns and create products that better align with customer demands.

One of Coca-Cola's most successful AI initiatives is its **Freestyle** vending machine, which allows consumers to create custom beverage combinations. The machine collects data on consumer preferences, which is then analyzed by AI to help Coca-Cola understand which flavor combinations are most popular. This data-driven approach to product development has resulted in the creation of new beverages that cater to evolving consumer tastes.

On the sustainability front, Coca-Cola has implemented AI-driven solutions to **reduce its environmental impact**. The company uses AI to optimize its supply chain, reducing waste and improving energy efficiency. By analyzing data on transportation routes, packaging materials, and production processes,

Coca-Cola has identified opportunities to reduce its carbon footprint and water usage. These efforts have resulted in a **10% reduction in greenhouse gas emissions** across the company's global operations.

Key Takeaways from AI-Driven Success Stories

The case studies highlighted in this chapter demonstrate the transformative power of AI across a wide range of industries. From manufacturing and healthcare to retail and renewable energy, AI has enabled organizations to optimize operations, reduce costs, and drive sustainability. Here are some key takeaways from these success stories:

1. **AI Drives Efficiency and Productivity**: Across industries, AI has been instrumental in improving operational efficiency and increasing productivity. By automating repetitive tasks and optimizing processes, AI frees up human workers to focus on higher-value activities.

2. **AI Supports Sustainability Goals**: Many organizations are using AI to reduce their environmental impact by optimizing resource usage, minimizing waste, and improving energy efficiency. AI-driven sustainability initiatives not only benefit the planet but also create long-term value for businesses.

3. **AI Enables Personalization and Innovation**: In industries such as retail and consumer goods, AI has enabled companies to gain deeper insights into customer preferences, allowing them to create personalized

experiences and innovate new products that meet evolving demands.

4. **Predictive Analytics Enhance Decision-Making**: AI-powered predictive analytics allow businesses to make smarter, data-driven decisions. Whether it's predicting equipment failures in manufacturing or forecasting demand in retail, AI enables organizations to stay ahead of challenges and opportunities.

Final Thoughts: As more companies embrace digital transformation, AI will continue to play a critical role in shaping the future of business and sustainability. The success stories highlighted in this chapter offer valuable lessons for organizations looking to harness the power of AI to achieve their goals.

Looking Ahead: As we conclude our journey, Chapter 19 will address the challenges that organizations often face when implementing AI. From cultural resistance to technical complexities, we'll explore practical strategies to overcome these barriers and ensure successful AI adoption. By understanding and addressing these challenges, you can pave the way for a smoother transition, unlocking the full potential of AI within your organization while building a resilient, future-ready foundation for growth.

20
Navigating the Challenges: Overcoming Barriers to AI Adoption

"Every challenge in transformation is an opportunity to lead with resilience."

Adopting **artificial intelligence (AI)** is no longer just a competitive advantage; it has become a strategic imperative for businesses looking to innovate, improve efficiency, and drive growth. However, despite its transformative potential, the journey to AI adoption is not without its challenges. From **budget constraints** and **skills gaps** to **organizational resistance** and concerns about privacy, companies face several hurdles that can slow down or prevent the successful implementation of AI technologies. In this chapter, we'll explore the common obstacles organizations encounter when adopting AI and provide actionable strategies to overcome these challenges.

1. Budget Constraints: Securing Resources for AI Investments

One of the most significant barriers to AI adoption is the **high upfront costs** associated with implementing AI technologies. From purchasing AI software and hardware to hiring skilled talent and training employees, the financial investment required for AI projects can be daunting for many businesses, especially small and medium-sized enterprises (SMEs).

In addition to the initial investment, there are ongoing costs related to **maintenance**, **data storage**, and **model updates**, which can strain an organization's budget. Without adequate resources, companies may struggle to scale their AI initiatives or achieve the desired outcomes from their investments.

Solution: Start Small and Scale Gradually

To overcome budget constraints, organizations should consider starting with **small-scale AI projects** that deliver quick wins and measurable ROI. By focusing on pilot programs or specific use cases—such as automating customer support with AI chatbots or improving sales forecasts with predictive analytics—businesses can demonstrate the value of AI before committing to larger investments.

Once the initial AI projects have proven successful, companies can gradually scale their AI initiatives by reinvesting the gains into further AI development. Additionally, businesses can explore partnerships with **AI vendors**, **cloud-based AI solutions**, or **open-source AI tools** to minimize upfront costs and reduce the financial burden.

Example: **Zappos**, an online retailer, began its AI journey by implementing **AI-powered chatbots** to automate customer service inquiries. The initial project was low-cost but provided a clear ROI in the form of reduced response times and improved customer satisfaction. After seeing success with this small-scale implementation, Zappos expanded its use of AI across its supply chain and inventory management processes.

2. Skills Gaps: Building an AI-Ready Workforce

Another common challenge for organizations adopting AI is the **lack of skilled talent** needed to develop, deploy, and maintain AI systems. AI requires expertise in areas such as **data science**, **machine learning**, **AI engineering**, and **cybersecurity**—skills that are in high demand but often in short supply. According to a **2024 Deloitte report**, **54% of companies** cite a shortage of AI talent as one of the top barriers to AI adoption.

The skills gap is particularly pronounced for companies in traditional industries where employees may not have experience working with advanced technologies. This lack of expertise can hinder the successful integration of AI into business processes, leading to delayed projects, increased costs, or underperforming AI systems.

Solution: Invest in Upskilling and Reskilling

To address the AI skills gap, organizations should prioritize **upskilling and reskilling** their workforce. By offering training programs, online courses, and workshops, companies can equip their existing employees with the necessary AI knowledge and technical skills. This not only reduces the need for external hiring but also fosters a culture of continuous learning and innovation within the organization.

Businesses can also consider partnering with **universities**, **AI training providers**, or **professional organizations** to develop tailored training programs that align with their AI goals. In addition to internal training, companies may benefit from **hiring AI consultants** or outsourcing certain AI projects to third-party experts while building in-house capabilities.

Example: **PwC** addressed the AI skills gap by launching its **Digital Accelerator Program**, which focuses on upskilling employees in AI, data analytics, and machine learning. Through this program, PwC has trained over **1,000 employees** to become AI specialists, enabling the firm to enhance its AI-driven services and solutions.

3. Resistance to Change: Fostering an AI-First Culture

Implementing AI technologies often requires a fundamental shift in how organizations operate, which can lead to **resistance to change** from employees and management alike. This resistance may stem from fears of job displacement, concerns about increased automation, or skepticism about AI's ability to deliver on its promises.

In some cases, employees may feel threatened by AI's potential to replace certain roles or may be uncomfortable adopting new tools and technologies that require additional training. Similarly, executives may be hesitant to invest in AI due to uncertainty about its long-term benefits or a lack of understanding of AI's capabilities.

Solution: Foster a Culture of Innovation and Collaboration

To overcome resistance to AI adoption, organizations must foster a **culture of innovation** that encourages experimentation, collaboration, and openness to new technologies. Leadership plays a critical role in driving this cultural shift—executives should **champion AI initiatives**, communicate the benefits of AI clearly, and involve employees in the process of AI integration.

By demonstrating how AI can enhance—not replace—existing roles, companies can alleviate employee concerns and build trust in AI technologies. For example, AI can automate repetitive tasks, allowing employees to focus on more strategic, creative, and high-value work. Providing employees with opportunities for **upskilling** and offering support during the transition to AI can further reduce resistance and ensure a smoother adoption process.

Example: **Shell** successfully navigated resistance to AI adoption by implementing a **digital transformation strategy** that prioritized employee engagement. The company launched an internal campaign to educate employees about the benefits of AI and how it would enhance their roles. Additionally, Shell offered

AI training programs to upskill its workforce, fostering a culture of collaboration and innovation.

4. Data Challenges: Ensuring Data Quality and Privacy

AI systems rely on large volumes of high-quality data to function effectively, but many organizations struggle with **data challenges** such as data silos, poor data quality, or concerns about **data privacy**. Without clean, well-organized, and accessible data, AI models may produce inaccurate results or fail to deliver meaningful insights.

Data privacy is another major concern, particularly with the rise of **data protection regulations** like the **General Data Protection Regulation (GDPR)** in Europe and the **California Consumer Privacy Act (CCPA)** in the United States. Organizations must ensure that their AI systems comply with these regulations and that they are handling sensitive customer data responsibly.

Solution: Implement Robust Data Governance and Privacy Practices

To address data challenges, organizations should establish a **comprehensive data governance framework** that ensures data is accurate, consistent, and secure. This involves investing in **data cleaning**, **data integration**, and **data management** tools that help break down silos and improve data accessibility across departments.

In addition, businesses should implement **privacy-by-design** principles when developing AI systems. This means embedding privacy and security measures into AI models from the outset, ensuring that data is anonymized, encrypted, and used in compliance with relevant regulations. By prioritizing data governance and privacy, organizations can build trust with customers and stakeholders, paving the way for successful AI adoption.

Example: **Procter & Gamble (P&G)** invested in a robust **data governance** strategy to ensure that its AI systems operate with high-quality, compliant data. The company implemented data integration tools that allowed it to break down data silos and ensure consistent data quality across its global operations. As a result, P&G was able to deploy AI-driven insights to optimize its supply chain and marketing efforts, improving operational efficiency and customer targeting.

5. Scaling AI: Moving from Pilots to Enterprise-Wide Deployment

While many companies successfully implement AI in pilot projects, they often struggle to scale these initiatives across the entire organization. The transition from pilot to full-scale AI deployment requires careful planning, significant investment, and the ability to integrate AI into existing workflows and systems.

Solution: Develop a Scalable AI Strategy

To scale AI effectively, businesses must develop a clear **AI strategy** that outlines how AI initiatives will be expanded across departments, regions, or functions. This strategy should include a roadmap for integrating AI with existing business systems and processes, as well as a plan for **cross-functional collaboration** between data scientists, IT teams, and business leaders.

In addition to building internal capabilities, companies may benefit from adopting **cloud-based AI platforms** or partnering with **AI-as-a-service providers** to scale their AI solutions more efficiently. These platforms offer the flexibility to deploy AI at scale without the need for significant upfront infrastructure investments.

Example: General Electric (GE) successfully scaled its AI initiatives by developing an enterprise-wide **digital transformation strategy**. GE deployed AI-driven predictive maintenance systems across its entire fleet of industrial equipment, reducing downtime and improving operational efficiency. By leveraging a cloud-based AI platform, GE was able to scale its AI solutions globally, achieving significant cost savings and productivity gains.

Final Thoughts: While the path to AI adoption is filled with challenges, businesses that proactively address these barriers will be well-positioned to reap the rewards of digital transformation. By focusing on **upskilling, fostering a culture of innovation**, implementing robust **data governance**, and developing a **scalable AI strategy**, organizations can overcome obstacles and unlock the full potential of AI technologies.

Looking Ahead: In the final chapter, we'll reflect on the transformative journey of AI and digital transformation and look towards the future. We'll explore emerging trends, potential challenges, and the evolving role of AI in shaping tomorrow's digital landscape. As we wrap up, this chapter will provide insights into how organizations can stay adaptive, innovative, and resilient as they navigate the dynamic road ahead. Join us for a forward-looking exploration of how AI will continue to drive and redefine digital transformation in the years to come.

21

The Road Ahead: The Future of AI-Driven Digital Transformation

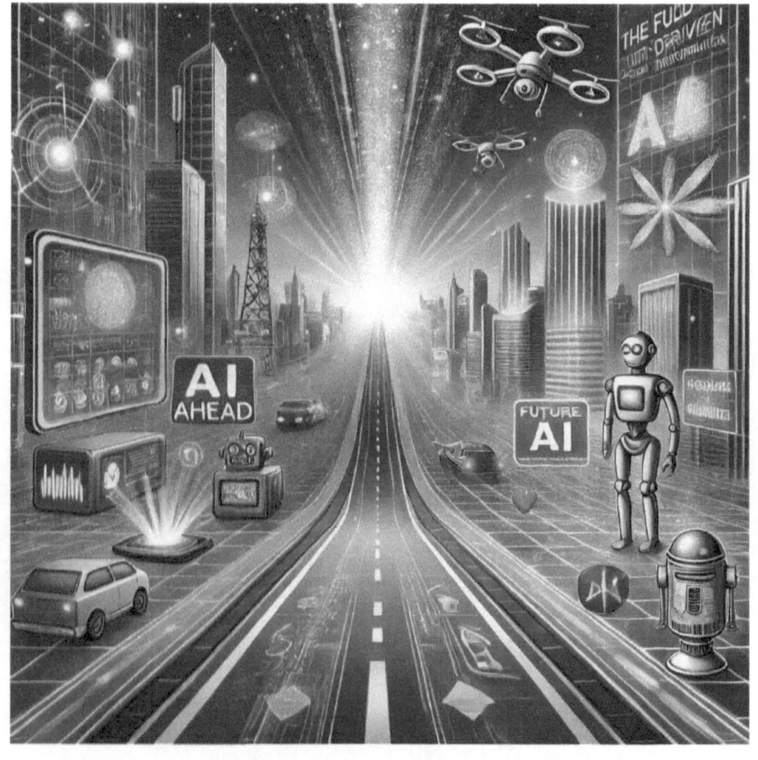

"The future of AI isn't a destination—it's a continuous journey of discovery."

As we look to the future, the fusion of **artificial intelligence (AI)** and **digital transformation** will continue to reshape industries, redefine how we live and work, and push the boundaries of technological innovation. AI has already revolutionized many sectors, but its full potential is yet to be realized. In this forward-looking chapter, we will explore upcoming trends in AI, anticipate the next frontier in technological evolution, and discuss how businesses can prepare for the future of **AI-driven digital transformation**.

1. The Rise of Autonomous AI Systems

One of the most significant trends we can expect to see in the coming years is the rise of **autonomous AI systems**. These systems, powered by advances in **deep learning** and **reinforcement learning**, will have the ability to make complex decisions and perform tasks without direct human intervention. Unlike traditional AI systems, which rely on predefined rules or human input, autonomous AI systems will be able to **learn**, **adapt**, and **evolve** in real time.

Autonomous AI systems will find applications in a wide range of industries, from **self-driving cars** and **autonomous drones** to **smart factories** and **AI-powered healthcare robots**. These systems will not only increase efficiency but also enable businesses to operate more **resiliently** in unpredictable environments.

Example: In manufacturing, **autonomous AI-driven robots** will be capable of performing complex assembly tasks, identifying and addressing problems in real time, and even collaborating with human workers to optimize production processes. By 2025, autonomous systems are expected to drive significant productivity gains in manufacturing, logistics, and other high-demand sectors.

2. AI-Driven Personalization at Scale

As AI continues to evolve, businesses will have the ability to deliver **hyper-personalized experiences** to customers on a massive scale. AI-driven personalization will extend beyond traditional marketing and customer service; it will become a core part of how businesses interact with customers in every aspect of their operations.

In retail, AI-powered **recommendation engines** will analyze individual customer preferences and behaviors to offer personalized products, services, and experiences. In healthcare, AI will enable personalized treatment plans based on genetic information, lifestyle, and real-time health data. Across industries, businesses will use AI to create customized experiences that resonate with individual customers, driving higher engagement and loyalty.

Example: **Netflix** and **Spotify** are early pioneers of AI-driven personalization, offering users tailored content recommendations based on their preferences. In the coming years, other industries will adopt similar AI techniques, enabling businesses to provide personalized offers and experiences at scale.

3. The Convergence of AI with Other Emerging Technologies

The next frontier of AI will be marked by its convergence with other emerging technologies such as **blockchain**, **5G**, the **Internet of Things (IoT)**, and **quantum computing**. Together, these technologies will amplify AI's potential, enabling new levels of connectivity, data processing power, and innovation.

For example, **5G** networks will provide the ultra-fast connectivity needed to support real-time AI applications in industries like autonomous vehicles, smart cities, and edge computing. **Blockchain technology** will enable secure, decentralized AI systems by allowing data to be shared transparently across multiple stakeholders without the risk of tampering. **Quantum computing**, still in its early stages, promises to dramatically increase AI's ability to process complex datasets and solve problems that are currently beyond the reach of classical computers.

Example: In the healthcare sector, the convergence of AI with **IoT** and **5G** will enable the development of real-time, remote patient monitoring systems. These systems will collect and analyze data from wearable devices, allowing healthcare providers to track patient health continuously and intervene when necessary.

4. AI and the Evolution of Ethical Standards

As AI becomes more integrated into our daily lives, the need for **ethical AI** will become more urgent. The future of AI will be defined not just by its capabilities, but by the ethical frameworks that guide its development and use. Ensuring that AI systems are **fair**, **transparent**, **accountable**, and **respectful of privacy** will be crucial in maintaining public trust and avoiding unintended consequences.

The concept of **responsible AI** will gain prominence, with organizations adopting robust **AI governance** frameworks to ensure that AI systems are designed and deployed ethically.

This will involve conducting bias audits, ensuring that AI systems are transparent and explainable, and complying with data protection regulations. We can also expect to see governments and regulatory bodies introduce new laws and standards for AI, aimed at ensuring that AI technologies are used in ways that benefit society while minimizing harm.

Example: The **European Union's AI Act**, set to be fully implemented by 2025, will introduce regulations governing the development and use of AI technologies in the region. The act will prioritize human rights, data privacy, and transparency, setting a global precedent for the ethical use of AI.

5. AI-Powered Sustainability and Green Innovation

As businesses become more committed to sustainability, AI will play a pivotal role in enabling **green innovation** and driving **environmental responsibility**. AI's ability to analyze complex data and optimize processes will help companies reduce their carbon footprint, minimize waste, and adopt more sustainable business practices.

In industries such as **energy**, **manufacturing**, and **agriculture**, AI will be used to optimize resource usage, improve energy efficiency, and manage supply chains sustainably. AI-powered **smart grids** will balance energy supply and demand, while **AI-driven predictive analytics** will help companies monitor and reduce emissions.

Example: **Google** has already pioneered AI-driven sustainability efforts by using its **DeepMind AI** to reduce the energy consumption of its data centers by 30%. As AI technologies continue to evolve, more businesses will use AI to develop eco-friendly innovations that contribute to global sustainability goals.

6. The Future of AI in the Workforce

As we discussed in previous chapters, AI will continue to reshape the workforce, automating repetitive tasks while augmenting human roles in more creative, strategic, and high-value activities. The future of work will involve a close collaboration between humans and AI, with workers using AI-driven tools to improve decision-making, productivity, and innovation.

Upskilling and **reskilling** will become essential for workers looking to thrive in the AI-powered economy. As new job roles emerge in fields like **AI ethics**, **machine learning engineering**, and **data science**, businesses and educational institutions will need to invest in workforce development programs that equip workers with the skills needed to succeed.

Example: In the **construction** industry, AI-driven robotics and **building information modeling (BIM)** will enhance productivity by automating routine tasks such as materials handling and structural analysis. Workers will be trained to operate AI-powered machines, focus on high-level project management, and use AI insights to make more informed decisions on-site.

7. The Democratization of AI

The next decade will also see the **democratization of AI**, with AI technologies becoming more accessible to organizations of all sizes, not just tech giants or large enterprises. Advances in **cloud computing**, **low-code/no-code AI platforms**, and **AI-as-a-**

Service will enable smaller businesses and startups to leverage AI without needing extensive technical expertise or significant financial resources.

By lowering the barriers to entry, AI democratization will foster a new wave of innovation across industries, empowering businesses to solve complex problems and develop new products and services using AI tools. As a result, AI will become a key enabler of entrepreneurship and economic growth in both developed and emerging markets.

Example: **Startups** and small businesses are increasingly adopting **no-code AI platforms** like **Akkio** and **Bubble**, which allow non-technical users to build and deploy AI models without writing code. This democratization of AI will enable businesses in sectors such as e-commerce, healthcare, and education to harness the power of AI for their specific needs.

Final Thoughts: Preparing for the AI-Driven Future - A Symphony of Minds & Machines

As we look ahead, it's clear that AI will continue to shape our industries, economies, and society, driving digital transformation on an unprecedented scale. To thrive in this evolving landscape, organizations must embrace a harmonious blend of human intelligence and AI—a *Symphony of Minds & Machines*. This synergy is essential not just for leveraging AI's capabilities, but for fostering a digital transformation that resonates with purpose and impact.

In this AI-driven world, success will require agility, innovation, and a steadfast commitment to responsible AI practices. By investing in upskilling, nurturing a culture of continuous learning, and aligning AI with strategic goals, businesses can unlock the transformative potential of this symphony. However, the path forward must be guided by ethical principles, ensuring that the benefits of AI are accessible, sustainable, and equitably shared.

The *Symphony of Minds & Machines* is not just about technology; it's about forging a collaborative future where human creativity and machine intelligence work in concert to drive meaningful change. Together, we can build a digital world where AI enhances our capabilities, respects our values, and advances society as a whole. As we navigate the future of AI-driven transformation, let us do so with purpose, harmony, and a vision for a world that serves the greater good.

Appendix: Acknowledgments and References

This book, **AI Fusion: Transforming the Digital World,** is the culmination of extensive research, collaboration, and insights drawn from a wide array of experts, organizations, and institutions at the forefront of artificial intelligence (AI) and digital transformation. Their contributions have been instrumental in shaping the discussions and case studies throughout these chapters. Here are the key acknowledgments and references, along with relevant websites for further exploration:

Acknowledgments

I extend my deepest gratitude to the following individuals, organizations, and institutions whose pioneering work has been foundational to the content presented in this book:

1. **Industry Leaders and Innovators**

   Many leading companies have been trailblazers in AI-driven innovation and digital transformation. Organizations like Google, IBM, Microsoft, Amazon, Siemens, and Unilever have provided invaluable case studies and real-world applications that demonstrate the transformative power of AI.

   o   Google: www.google.com

   o   IBM: www.ibm.com

- o   Microsoft: www.microsoft.com

- o   Amazon: www.amazon.com

- o   Siemens: www.siemens.com

- o   Unilever: www.unilever.com

2. **Academic Institutions and Research Organizations**

Institutions like MIT, Stanford University, and Carnegie Mellon University have laid the groundwork for many AI and digital transformation strategies discussed in this book. Their research in AI, machine learning, and ethics has been crucial in shaping the framework for responsible AI use.

- o   MIT: www.mit.edu

- o   Stanford University: www.stanford.edu

- o   Carnegie Mellon University: www.cmu.edu

3. **AI and Ethics Thought Leaders**

The ethical dimensions of AI are pivotal to its adoption. Organizations such as the AI Ethics Institute, Partnership on AI, and the European Union's AI Act have led the way in creating frameworks that ensure AI is developed and used responsibly.

- o   AI Ethics Institute: www.aiethicsinstitute.org

- o   Partnership on AI: www.partnershiponai.org

- o   European Union AI Act: www.eur-lex.europa.eu

4. **Contributors to AI Policy and Governance**

The European Union and other governmental bodies have been instrumental in defining the regulatory landscape for AI. Their efforts in governance have highlighted both the opportunities and challenges of AI's role in digital transformation.

- European Union: www.europa.eu

References

The insights in this book are drawn from authoritative sources, research papers, and real-world case studies. Key references include:

1. **World Economic Forum (2024)** – Insights on AI-driven job creation, workforce trends, and upskilling strategies.

    Available at: www.weforum.org/reports/ai-job-market -2024

2. **McKinsey & Company (2023)** – Perspectives on digital transformation strategies and AI adoption.

    Available at: www.mckinsey.com/insights/ai-digital-transformation

3. **PwC (2023)** – Analysis of AI's role in sustainability and reducing carbon footprints.

    Available at: www.pwc.com/ai-sustainability-report

4. **Deloitte (2024)** – Research on AI skills gaps and workforce readiness for digital transformation.

    Available at: www.deloitte.com/global-ai-skills-gap-report

5. **International Energy Agency (IEA) (2024)** – Data on AI's impact on global energy efficiency.

    Available at: www.iea.org/reports/ai-energy-sustainability

6. **MIT Technology Review** – Articles on ethical AI, transparency, and responsible AI challenges.

Available at: www.technologyreview.com/ai-ethics-transparency

7. **Forrester Research (2024)** – AI's influence on customer experience in retail and finance.

   Available at: www.forrester.com/research/ai-personalization

8. **Gartner (2024)** – Insights on AI market trends, cybersecurity, and enterprise applications.

   Available at: www.gartner.com/en/insights/ai-digital-transformation

9. **European Union AI Act (2025)** – Guidelines for AI governance within the EU.

   Available at: www.eur-lex.europa.eu/ai-act-2025

Additional Sources

For those interested in delving deeper into AI and digital transformation, the following additional references were also influential:

- **"AI Superpowers" by Kai-Fu Lee** – A comparison of AI's global impact, highlighting competition between the U.S. and China.

  Available at: www.aisuperpowers.com

- **"Human + Machine" by Paul R. Daugherty and H. James Wilson** – An exploration of how AI and human collaboration drives productivity.

  Available at: www.humanmachinebook.com

- **"The Fourth Industrial Revolution" by Klaus Schwab**
  – A look at how AI and other technologies are reshaping economies and societies.

  Available at: www.weforum.org/reports/the-fourth-industrial-revolution

Author's Note

While this book draws on a substantial body of knowledge from leading experts and organizations, the perspectives, interpretations, and conclusions presented here are entirely my own. It has been a privilege to share the latest trends, case studies, and insights from both my experiences and the contributions of pioneers in AI-driven innovation. I am deeply grateful for the foundational work of those who have paved the way in this field. I encourage readers to explore the rich, evolving world of AI and digital transformation by engaging with the original sources referenced throughout this book, thereby deepening their understanding of this dynamic landscape.

About the Author

Kishor Narayanan Chiyyarath, is a seasoned **people, process, and technology transformation expert** with extensive experience in software development, technology management, and organizational development. Over the course of his career, Kishor has developed profound expertise in a wide array of globally recognized methodologies and frameworks, including CMMI (Capability Maturity Model Integration), ITIL® (Information Technology Infrastructure Library), PMP (Project Management Professional), PRINCE2® (Projects IN Controlled Environments), ISMS (Information Security Management System), DevOps, Agile & Scrum, as well as various International Standards such as ISO, and Best Management Practices.

Kishor's deep understanding of these frameworks has enabled him to lead and contribute to numerous innovative projects across diverse organizations. His work has been instrumental in streamlining processes, enhancing efficiency, and achieving strategic goals. He has significantly influenced the implementation of best management practices and the development of robust technology solutions that align seamlessly with organizational objectives.

Beyond his expertise in traditional technology management, Kishor is deeply passionate about the transformative power of **Artificial Intelligence (AI)** and **Data Science**, recognizing their potential to revolutionize industries and improve lives. However, he is equally committed to the ethical considerations surrounding **responsible AI development**, emphasizing the importance of balancing **innovation** with **accountability**. His advocacy extends to **Sustainability** and **Green AI**, ensuring that technological advancements are pursued with **environmental stewardship** and long-term societal benefits in mind. In *AI Fusion: Transforming the Digital World*, Kishor explores the profound synergy between **human intelligence** and **AI technologies**, emphasizing how **data, computing power**, and **responsible AI adoption** are reshaping industries. His insights into **Green AI** and **responsible computing** reflect his vision for a **sustainable technological future**—one where innovation drives **business success** while prioritizing **ethical practices** and **environmental consciousness**.

A dedicated advocate for continuous learning and improvement, Kishor is committed to helping organizations achieve excellence by aligning technological advancements with strategic business goals. His work is guided by a deep belief in the transformative power of technology to drive business success, foster sustainability, and create a better future.